Road to Destruction offers a unique visual insight into the climactic Battle of Stalingrad during the autumn and winter of 1942–43. Pushing forward through the southern steppes aiming to capture the vital Caucasian oilfields, before being caught up in some of the most vicious street fighting known in military history, the German 6th Army was bled white and ultimately destroyed.

The author has drawn on a wide selection of rare and mostly previously unpublished photographs accompanied by in-depth captions to provide a superb photographic history of this key turning point in the Second World War.

The images reveal the unfolding story, through the hopeful beginnings and major successes at the beginning of operations, as German forces cut a rapid swathe towards the oilfields. By early autumn 1942, the Germans were seemingly on the brink of success as they reached the banks of the Volga and the vitally important city of Stalingrad. Yet the Red Army dug extremely deep, and relying on grim determination, courage and resourcefulness, fought bitterly. The German advance was slowed to a crawl, as incredibly bitter hand-to-hand fighting took place throughout the city. The situation for the German troops became worse and worse, winter set in, and with it major Soviet counter-attacks. By late November 1942 the situation was worsening for the Germans fighting at Stalingrad. Completely encircled, Soviet forces slowly closed in as the vicious winter took hold, and the Luftwaffe's air support operations became increasingly ineffective. The remnants of 6th Army surrendered in February, shadows of the troops that had advanced across the steppes the previous summer. In all, the horrendous fighting resulted in more than 1.5 million casualties on both sides.

An important visual record of one of history's greatest and most bitterly fought battles.

About the author

Ian Baxter is a military historian who specialises in German twentieth century military history. He has written more than twenty books including *Into the Abyss: The Last Years of the Waffen-SS, From Retreat to Defeat: The Last Years of the German Army on the Eastern Front, Operation Bagration – The Destruction of Army Group Centre 1944, Poland – The Eighteen Day Victory March, Panzers In North Africa, The Red Army At Stalingrad,* and *German Guns of the Third Reich*, as well as contributing over 100 articles to a range of well-known military periodicals. He currently lives in Essex with Michelle and son Felix.

ROAD TO DESTRUCTION

OPERATION BLUE AND THE BATTLE OF STALINGRAD 1942–43

A Photographic History

Ian Baxter

Helion & Company Ltd

Helion & Company Limited
26 Willow Road
Solihull
West Midlands
B91 1UE
England
Tel. 0121 705 3393
Fax 0121 711 4075
Email: publishing@helion.co.uk
Website: http://www.helion.co.uk

Published by Helion & Company 2008

Designed and typeset by Helion & Company Limited, Solihull, West Midlands
Cover designed by Bookcraft Limited, Stroud, Gloucestershire
Printed by Cromwell Press Ltd, Trowbridge, Wiltshire

ISBN 978 1 906033 15 6

British Library Cataloguing-in-Publication Data.
A catalogue record for this book is available from the British Library.

For details of other military history titles published by Helion & Company Limited contact the above address, or visit our website: http://www.helion.co.uk.

We always welcome receiving book proposals from prospective authors.

Contents

Photographic Acknowledgements vi

Introduction vii

Prelude to Destruction

History of the German 6th Army in Russia 1941–42 8

Assessment of the German Soldier 9

Part I – Operation Blue

Road to Hell 11

Volga Reached 12

Part II – Siege of Stalingrad

Bitter Fighting 41

Into the Cauldron 43

Operation Uranus 45

Entombment. 47

Part III – The Fall of Stalingrad

Desperation 89

Attacking the *Kessel* 91

Destruction of 6th Army 93

Epilogue 116

Appendices

I   German personal equipment and weapons 117

II   German infantry battalion 1941–42 118

III Combat chronology of German 6th Army Eastern Front 1941–42 119

IV German 6th Army Order of Battle 1942 121

V   Soviet Orders of Battle 124

Bibliography 125

Photographic Acknowledgements

It is with the greatest pleasure that I use this opportunity on concluding this book to thank those who helped make this volume possible. My expression of gratitude first goes to my German photographic collector Rolf Halfen. He has been an unfailing source; supplying me with a number of photographs that were obtained from numerous private sources. Throughout the research stage of this book Rolf searched and contacted numerous collectors all over Germany, trying to find a multitude of interesting and rare photographs.

Further afield in Poland I am also extremely grateful to Marcin Kaludow, my Polish photographic specialist, who supplied me with a great variety photographs that he sought from private photographic collections in Poland, Russia and the Ukraine.

Introduction

Road to Destruction is a unique insight into the last six months of the German 6th Army. Drawing on rare and previously unpublished photographs accompanied by in-depth captions, the book is an absorbing analysis of the 6th Army's march to Stalingrad during the summer of 1942. It reveals in detail how the 6th Army, which was the largest German army on the Eastern Front, was ordered to make a determined drive through the vastness of southern Russia to a city that carried Stalin's name. For the soldiers of the 6th Army, the name Stalingrad bore no real significance, other than that it was a city that marked the end of an exhausting and costly summer offensive. When the 6th Army arrived on the western banks of the great Volga River, poised to attack the city, no one believed that the Russians were resolved at turning Stalingrad into a formidable centre of resistance. What followed in the late summer of 1942 was a momentous conflict and the bloodiest battle in the history of warfare. The fighting was said to have equalled the horrors of the battle of Verdun during the First World War. However, unlike Verdun where either side annihilated each other by long range machine gun fire or artillery, in the city of Stalingrad the battles were fought separately between individuals, often across the street, where fighting was frequently settled by hand-to-hand duels among the rubble and burning buildings. Although many of the soldiers were hardened veterans that had experienced urbanized fighting before in Russia, nothing could possibly have compared the horrors that they were about to experience. In less than five months the battle cost the lives of nearly two million people. What follows is the story of the 6th Army's march to Stalingrad, the battle that ensued, and its ultimate destruction.

Prelude to Destruction

History of the 6th Army in Russia 1941–1942

All along the Eastern Front, the glare from thousands of gun flashes lit the eastern dawn on 22 June 1941. From their jump-off positions, the German Army, all three million of them, began their greatest attack in military history. 'Barbarossa' – the code word for the invasion of the Soviet Union had begun in earnest.

For this monumental attack against Russia the Germans had divided their forces into three Army Groups: North, under Field Marshal Ritter von Leeb; Centre, under Field Marshal Fedor von Bock; and South, under Field Marshal Gerd von Rundstedt. The Panzer forces which had been so successful in Poland and France were kept separate from the infantry and concentrated in four independent *Gruppen*, under the skilful command of Guderian, Hoth, Hoepner and Kleist. They had three objectives, Leningrad, Moscow and the Ukraine. The Panzer forces were to smash the Russian Army, whilst the infantry and artillery, following in the wake of the armoured spearheads, were to force the enemy's surrender. It was made clear from the beginning of the invasion that under no circumstances were these forces to be embroiled in heavy urbanized fighting. The Red Army was to be surrounded by devastating superiority and then destroyed. It was going to be another Blitzkrieg victory, but on an immense scale.

On the Southern Front Rundstedt's German infantry divisions with some six hundred tanks distributed among them, bulldozed its way through thinly held Russian defences. The main thrust in the south was directed between the southern edge of the Pripet Marshes and the foothills of the Carpathian Mountains. Here Rundstedt concentrated the whole of the 1st Panzer Army, 6th Army, and 17th Army. The 6th Army, under the faithful command of Field Marshal von Reichenau, consisted of three Army Corps, XVII, XVII, XXXXIV and one reserve – the LV Army Corps. Reichenau had commanded the 6th Army during the battle of France in 1940, but the army had already made a name for itself during the invasion of Poland. On the Eastern Front the 6th Army once again completely mastered the enemy despite being continually harassed by strong Russian forces that had been cut off in the wooded swampland between the Pripet Marshes and the Carpathian Mountains. As the 6th Army pushed on towards the Dnieper River its primary task was to hold onto as much ground as possible and prevent all intact retreating enemy formations from withdrawing deep into Russia. Over the days and weeks that followed the speed of the 6 Armee was multiplied tenfold by the mobility of the Southern Army Group's armour as it rammed and overran enemy obstacles. Again and again the Russians were overwhelmed by the German onslaught. By August the 6th Army had swung out east of Kiev as German forces began mopping up the last remnants in and around the besieged city. When the battle of Kiev finally ended on 21 September 1941 almost 665,000 Russian troops had been captured in the encirclement. Exhilarated by the fall of Kiev, the 6th Army pushed mercilessly forward leaving a trail of devastation in its wake. Across the whole of Reichenau's front, tanks hammered deeper and the guns of the infantry divisions lengthened their range. For the troops of the 6th Army it seemed that Blitzkrieg had once again been imprinted on the battlefield and there was an aura of invincibility among the men. Yet much of the 6th Army was not mechanized. There were some 25,000 horses alone that were used to move guns and supplies. Although this type of transportation did not cause its commanders initial concern, by the time the army arrived at the higher Donets River in October 1941 the weather began to change. Cold, driving rain fell on the Army Group's front and within hours the Russian countryside had been turned into a quagmire with roads and fields becoming virtually impassable. Many of the roads leading to the Caucasus via the city of Rostov had become boggy swamps. Although tanks and other tracked vehicles managed to push through the mire at a slow pace, animal draught, trucks and other wheeled vehicles became hopelessly stuck in deep boggy mud. To make matters worse during November the German supply lines became increasingly over-stretched, their vehicles were breaking down, and casualty returns were mounting. Stiff resistance too began to hinder progress. As the situation deteriorated further Rundstedt, against Hitler's orders, ordered Kleist's 1st Panzer Army to evacuate Rostov and fall back over the Mius River, some 60 miles west of the city. On the night of 30 November Rundstedt was relieved of his command and replaced by Reichenau. A few days later a forty-three year old staff officer called Friedrich Wilhelm Ernst Paulus was promoted to command of the 6th Army. For some time Paulus had been wanting a field post, and was elated when he received his new assignment. On 1 January 1942, he was promoted to General of Panzer Troops and took up his new command four days later. As a commander Paulus was a truly proficient fastidious staff officer, but he lacked decisiveness, and regarded the *Führer* as a flawless military expert.

Paulus directed his first battle as commander of the 6th Army along the Dnieper River in the area around Dnepropetrovsk. It was here, in freezing temperatures, that Army Group South halted strong Soviet attacks and brought the winter offensive in the southern sector to a grinding halt. Both sides were totally exhausted following weeks of ceaseless fighting. Whilst the front lines stagnated the 6th Army engaged in a race of supplies.

On 9 May the German lines once more erupted in flame and smoke as the Russian unleashed a spring attack at Volchansk. The main strike came three days later when 640,000 men and 1,200 tanks from Timoshenko's Ukrainian Front attacked the 6th Army and hurled it back toward Kharkov. On 15 May Red Army forces threatened to envelope the city from the north and south. Paulus's 6th Army was severely battered by the overwhelming ferocity of the enemy as it tried frantically to hold its merge positions. Paulus had only ten infantry divisions, a Hungarian light division, and a Slovak artillery regiment. For almost two days these forces were subjected to heavy and incessant attacks until the 1st Panzer and 17th Armies were able to relieve the pressure. On 20 May Paulus was able to counterattack east of Kharkov and within a few days successfully linked up with Kleist west of the city, and encircled the main Russian striking force.

The success at Kharkov ignited a new optimism throughout the ranks of the German Army. Paulus received the Knight's Cross for his part in the victory, and a number of other commanders were decorated too. Although the Red Army had made a formidable impression on Paulus he was nonetheless convinced, as was his *Führer*, that victory in the south would be secured. Yet, even as his troops pulled out east of Kharkov to take part in the drive to Voronezh and the clearing operations of the Don, he never envisaged that the first seeds were being sewn of something more terrible than anything his troops had ever experienced.

Assessment of the German Soldier

When the German soldier ventured out across into Russia when 'Barbarossa' was first unleashed, the Red Army were a complete enigma to him. There was little information supplied about the country in which they were invading, nor was there anything substantial on the terrain and climate. He simply saw the Russians as Slavic people that were an inferior race. Propaganda had given the impression that all Russians were living in poverty and its antiquated army was totally unprepared for war. Even when the German soldier rolled across into Russia during the summer months of 1941, he was totally unaware of the immense undertaking he had in crushing the enemy. Although the ordinary German found a huge contrast between his own country and that in which he was fighting, they were totally unprepared for the unimaginable size and distance in which they had to march. The soldiers were amazed by the immense forests, the huge expanses of marshland, and the many rivers that were continuously prone to flooding. They were also surprised that the little information they did have, was often incorrect. Maps frequently showed none of the roads, and when they were fortunate enough to come across them, they were in such terrible state of repair that military traffic would often reduce them to nothing more than dirt tracks.

Another great contrast that the German soldier experienced during his march through Russia was the climatic conditions. There were extreme differences in temperature with the bitter cold sometimes dropping to thirty or even forty degrees below zero, and the terrible heat of the summer when temperatures soared to insufferable levels. When the first snow showers arrived in October 1941, the German soldier was totally unprepared for a Russian winter. Sleet and the cold driving rain turned the Russian countryside into a bog. The lack of winter clothing too caused widespread worry for the soldiers as they knew that the winter would create graver problems than the Russians themselves. By late 1941 supplies of winter clothing began to be delivered to the front, but many soldiers did not receive their garments until the first half of 1942. In an attempt to restore morale among the soldiers, which had been lost due to the harsh winter conditions of 1941/42, the army produced a winter warfare handbook. This book was primarily designed to assure the German soldier that they could deal with the arctic conditions, and a special chapter was written dealing with clothing and food. During 1942 various items of clothing were designed and introduced to help combat the Russian climate and increase the survivability of the German soldier on the battlefield.

Throughout 1942 the German soldier slowly adapted to the Russian climate and terrain, and was seen wearing a host of new summer and winter camouflage uniforms and newly designed steel helmets and field caps. Even the Panzer uniforms were being replaced. But despite the drastic measures implemented in the design of better uniforms and equipment in order to sustain the German soldier on the battlefield, nothing could mask the fact that they were up against an enemy that was numerically superior and fiercely contested every foot of ground to the death. To make matters worse the terrain also heavily influenced the conduct of military operations, especially for the German soldier of the 6th Army as he marched across seemingly unending expanses of flat terrain, sometimes encountering bitter opposition along the way. Here in the south the Germans had the greatest area to clear. Although the vast steppes were regarded as good tank country they lacked drinking water, and many soldiers suffered as a result. Yet despite the hardships that each man encountered along the way he was determined to fulfil his duty, reach the river Volga, and capture a little-known city called Stalingrad.

PART I

Operation Blau

Road to Hell

By the spring of 1942 Hitler, who was now in full command, was determined to smash the Red Army once and for all in southern Russia. An ambitious plan was worked out that involved the seizure of Stalingrad, and the isthmus between the Don and the Volga. Following the capture of Stalingrad he planned using the city as an anchor and sending the mass of his panzer force south to occupy the Caucasus, where it would be used to cut off vital Russian oil supplies. The operation was called 'Operation Blau'. The directive that Hitler himself dictated was executed in two stages. The first part of the summer operation was a determined all-out drive in successive enveloping thrusts along the Kursk-Voronezh axis, where it was to destroy the Soviet southern flank and carry on to the Don River. The second part was the advance to Stalingrad and across the lower Don into the Caucasus. For this operation Army Group South would be divided. He ordered General List's Army Group A to go south, toward Rostov and the Caucasus, while General Weichs's Army Group B would be responsible for the drive across the lower Don to the Volga and into Stalingrad.

In the regrouping Army Group B took command of the 2nd Panzer Army, 4th Panzer Army, and 6th Army. The first two were detached from Army Group Centre. Army Group A was assigned with the 1st Panzer Army, 11th, and 17th Armies. In order to support the drive to the Volga, Italy, Hungary and Rumania took to the field. Though these allied forces were under-equipped and badly trained, they were nonetheless helpful in bolstering the German forces in the area. For the summer offensive a number of divisions, especially those spearheading the drive were brought to authorized strength levels and this included artillery, anti-tank and anti-aircraft weapons as well. German strength in the air was equalled to that of the 1941 campaign with 1,500 aircraft of the total 2,750 being sent to the southern sector of the front.

As they stood poised to unleash their forces through southern Russia to the western banks of the Volga, it seemed that the Germans now held the upper hand. At dawn on 28 June 1942, the 2nd and 4th Panzer Armies opened up the 'Blau' offensive. Almost immediately the panzers smashed their way through lines of Red Army defences and drove at breakneck speed east of Kursk and pushed toward Voronezh, reaching the outskirts of the smouldering city in four days. Following the capture of the city 4th Panzer then swung southeast along the Don where it met with Paulus's 6th Army east of Kharkov. Over the next few weeks strung out over more than two-hundred miles the 6th Army with 20 divisions (250,000 men, 500 panzers, 7,000 guns and mortars, and 25,000 horses) pushed down towards the Don corridor on Stalingrad. The tremendous distances which these divisions had to cover could only be achieved by long foot marches. Due to the lack of adequate rail and road links, natural obstacles such as the *balka*, which were high, steep-sided, dried-up watercourses often obstructed the advance of a tank column until a diversion was made or a bridge erected. In some areas of the advance it was hampered by the lack of fuel, which had been temporarily diverted to Army Group A. Nonetheless, despite the problems that faced the 6th Army's advance during the first half of July it made moderately good progress.

On 17 July two of Paulus's divisions entered the town of Bobovskaya on the upper Chir. Hitler then immediately ordered that the 6th Army move to the Don bend and hamper any enemy forces that were preparing to build defences west of the Volga. A few days later Paulus received another order from the *Führer* to take the 6th Army to Stalingrad and capture it by high-speed assault. Paulus, however, did not have adequate reinforcements. His troops had been marching continuously for almost two weeks and were totally exhausted. But nonetheless he made a determined effort to drive out defences of the 62nd and 64th Soviet armies. In some areas there was bitter opposition and the Russians managed to hold Serafimovich and Kremenskaya. Although Russian resistance was occasionally patchy and disorganized again and again their units fought superbly and to the death. Once more German troops found themselves unexpectedly heavily engaged. Tormented by stiff opposition some units were barely able to maintain cohesion, and were soon repulsed by skillfully deployed

Russian soldiers. All along the German front, to the east, erupted into flame. Virtually everywhere flashes of gunfire merged into sheets of fire. A number of areas were ablaze as artillery, mortars, and tanks smashed into ear-splitting life. Across selected terrain, panzers led across open fields. As they approached enemy emplacements they allowed the infantry to overtake them and sweep in against anti-tank guns, before the tanks themselves once again took over. The Russians had once more proved to be fearless defenders and this was particularly true of the anti-tank gun crews that played a key role in combating German armour.

On 25 July another crises developed as the XIV Panzer Corps run out of fuel and reluctantly halted northeast of Kalach. Whilst waiting for fuel sixty Russian tanks cut the road behind them, and two hundred tanks attacked the 3rd and 60th Motorized divisions. The Russians immediately attacked the panzers and what followed was a violent and bloody battle with a number of German units being mauled and battered. Initially the situation looked dire for the Germans but as normal their reaction was quick and they managed to repel their irrepressible foe. As for the 6th Army they were now forced to try and consolidate enough strength to push forward and commit their whole army against Stalingrad. Paulus was directed to clear away Red Army forces deployed west of the Don. They would then press onto the great Volga River into Stalingrad where they were convinced they would triumph.

Volga Reached

Hitler's controversial Directive No.45, codenamed 'Brunswick', had directed Paulus's 6th Army, supported by General Hoth's 4th Panzer Army, which was dispatched from the Caucasus, to thrust forward to the city of Stalingrad, destroy all enemy forces, occupy the city and then block enemy communications between the Don and Volga. For the soldiers of the 6th and 4th Armies, the name Stalingrad bore no real significance, other than it was a city that would mark the end of a very costly summer offensive. To Hitler, however, Stalingrad was more than just a military objective; it bore the name of his old arch-enemy. For him it was a kind of contest between the Soviet dictator and himself. He regarded the city as an 'incubator' of Bolshevism, and despised it for the birth place where in 1918 Stalin, Budenny, Timoshenko and Voroshilov had defied Trotsky over his policy of war against the Whites, which eventually saw Stalin rise to power. Hitler was confident of capturing the city, but the Russians were equally determined to defend it at all costs. For the Soviets the time had come for every comrade and citizen to draw his teeth and finally prevent the deadly enemy from obtaining any more ambitious plans in the east. Already millions of soldiers and civilians had perished, and although the Russians had suffered the highest casualties, their devotion to the 'Motherland', and their determination and courage to halt the German crusade continued with fanatical violence. Thus, by late August 1942, at the news that the German forces on the Don were poised to strike across to the west bank of the Volga, the Russians began frantically making preparations not to evacuate the area, but to defend their beloved city with every drop of blood.

Finally around midday on 22 August 1942, soldiers of the 6th Army had completed the pontoon bridges across the Don. Tanks, halftracks, self-propelled assault guns, dozens of trucks and reconnaissance vehicles from General Hube's 16th Panzer Division rattled remorselessly across the broad expanse of water onto the east bank. Early the following morning Count von Strachwitz's *Abteilung* of the 2nd Panzer Regiment, reinforced with Panzergrenadier companies, advanced forward from the Don towards the Volga. As they drove eastwards, churning up huge dust clouds panzer crews could be seen standing fearlessly in their turrets waving their companies forward across the hot and dusty dry steppe. For these men of the 6th Army it was an historic moment, one their *Führer* would be proud of.

The drive towards the Volga was almost unhindered by the enemy, but as the forward elements of the army approached the river it was unexpectedly targeted by artillery batteries manned by young Russian girls. What followed was a series of close quarter fights. Once the batteries had more or less been silenced the battering ram of the 16th Panzer Division continued pushing forward. By about four in the afternoon on 23 August, the division finally reached the banks of the Volga, north of Stalingrad. For these men, gazing at the fast flowing river, these were glorious days for the German frontline regiments. With the warmth of the sun now on their backs many could now lay to rest the nightmares of the previous winter. Even some of the more pessimistic commanders that were seen surveying the far shore of the Volga through binoculars, were watching in awe as columns of black smoke rising from the heavy Luftwaffe raids on Stalingrad. Many were struck with a firm belief that more victories were beckoning. But already the whole region around Stalingrad had prepared itself for the defence of the city, and the incessant air attacks alone would not destroy its defences. All available men, women and children, nearly 200,000 of them, were mobilized in labour columns. Younger children were also put to work building earth walls on the banks of the Volga. Girls manned the many anti-aircraft batteries, and factories still open were

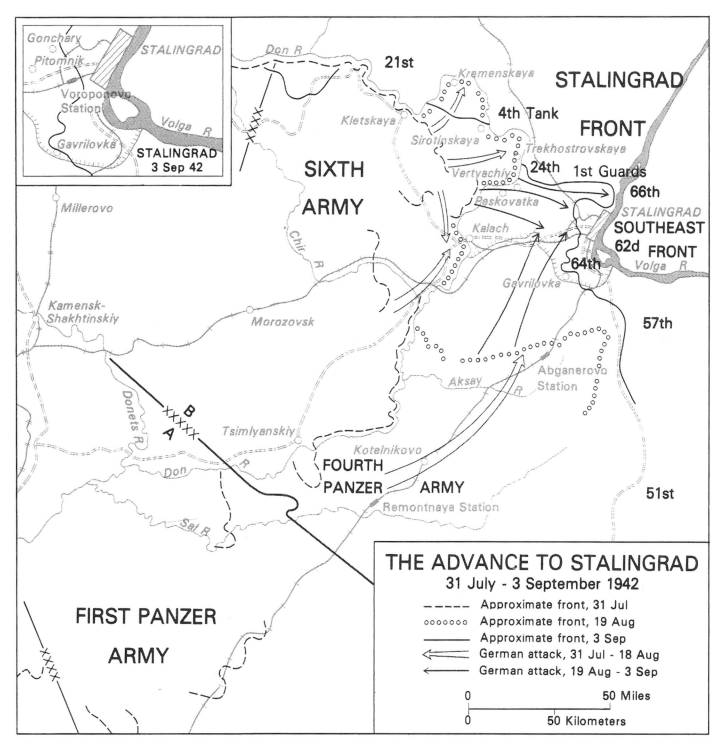

The Advance to Stalingrad 31 July-3 September 1942
(map appears courtesy of the Center of Military History United States Army, and originally appeared on page 383 of
Moscow to Stalingrad: Decision in the East by Earl F. Ziemke & Magna E. Bauer, 1987)

defended by industrial workers. Determined to hold the city to the death, the Soviet government was now staking the whole Russian campaign at the feet of Stalingrad. To its people it proclaimed a state of siege:

Comrades and citizens of Stalingrad! We shall never surrender our city to the depredations of the German invader. Each one of us must apply himself to the task of defending our beloved town, our home, and our families. Let us barricade every street; turn every district, every block, every house, into an impregnable fortress.

Every Russian left behind in Stalingrad was determined to fight in front of, and if necessary die inside the sewers, factories and wooden buildings of the city. Even after the terrible Luftwaffe raids which killed more than 40,000 of the city's inhabitants in one week, and turned many acres of the city, including stretches of the Volga shore into a burned and devastated wasteland of death, they still remained resolute into adapting Stalingrad into a formidable centre of resistance.

Whilst the Luftwaffe pounded the city, the 16th Panzer Division began digging in along the banks of the Volga. Later that evening the Germans shelled targets in the river and made plans to attack the city.

Stalingrad was a city of more than 500,000 people, and was constructed on the west bank of the Volga. It was twelve miles long, but just over two miles wide. It was the third largest industrial city in Russia. The huge tractor plants had been converted to produce more than a quarter of the country's tanks and armoured vehicles. There was a gun factory, metallurgical and chemical works, railroads, and oil tank farms. On the river itself the Russians used the main route for shipment of oil from the Caucasus. Strategically Stalingrad was no Moscow, but to the Germans success of the summer campaign could not be claimed without its capture. Paulus for one thought it was an easy target.

Early on the 24 August 1942, eager to smash through into Stalingrad 'Group Drumpen' of the 16th Panzer Division launched an attack against Spartakovka, north of the industrial part of the city. The Germans expected an easy victory, but as they pushed through along the northern outskirts of the burning city they were immediately repulsed by strong Russian resistance. A number of panzers then attempted to storm the city from the west, but they were soon halted by Russian tanks and infantry.

The Red Army's main objective was to try and force the Germans to abandon their corridor between the Don and Volga. Over the next few days they made a number of concerted attacks against the 6th Army dug in along the shores. Russian artillery shelling and fighter aircraft attacks were particularly heavy. Conditions in the German trenches had deteriorated quickly, and when it rained almost continuously on 29 August their improvised shelters soon filled with water. Only days earlier these soldiers had been elated by being the first to reach the river. Now they were crouched in filthy conditions among shattered trees and smouldering craters. It was a miserable existence, yet the worst was still to come.

A photograph taken just prior to 'Operation Blue' showing a stationary halftrack armed with a 3.7cm flak gun, which is concealed beneath tarpaulin. On the folding sides of the halftrack additional magazines for the gun could be carried. Note the single axle trailer on tow. This normally carried vital equipment including ammunition.

An artillery battery moves forward across the vast Russian steppe in late June 1942. During 'Operation Blue' the bulk of the artillery was pulled by animal draught. Quite frequently horse drawn artillery took much longer to transport its weaponry from one position to another.

A quadruple-barrelled self-propelled flak gun which is mounted on the rear of a halftrack has halted out in the steppe during 6th Army's march through southern Russia in late June 1942. The crew have used straw to camouflage the vehicle and parts of the gun from aerial view.

Panzers and halftrack personnel carriers belonging to *Panzergruppe* Kleist of the 1st *Panzer* Army, as it advances on Stalingrad in the summer of 1942. The 1st *Panzer* Army was designated to Army Group A and composed of the 3rd *Panzer*, 2nd Motorized Infantry, 7th German and 4th Romanian infantry divisions and Group Ruoff made up of 17th Army, which consisted of the 1st *Panzer*, one motorized infantry, 6th German and 4 Romanian infantry divisions, and the 8th Italian Army.

An artillery tractor moves across the steppe. The hinged sides and rear railings of the vehicle could be removed to allow extra space on board the halftrack and to provide a wider firing platform for the gunners when the tractor was in action against aerial or ground targets.

An unusual photograph showing an artillery unit using cows to tow its artillery. Maintaining the momentum of an advance was vital to success and, with transport, the whole advance might stall. For this reason the Germans utilised whatever they could from animal draught, trucks to tracked vehicles to tow or carry artillery to the forward edge of the battlefield.

Here infantry follow a StuG.III assault gun across a field during the opening phase of 'Blue'. Note the soldier in the foreground with an aluminium machine gun cartridge case and a man carrying a metal container on his back holding rounds for the

Laying next to their artillery tractor most of the crew try to rest during their arduous journey across southern Russia. Foliage has been draped over parts of the vehicle in order to conceal its distinctive shape from the air. Most of the steppe was covered by endless wheat fields and the lack of terrain features often made land navigation difficult.

A MG–34 machine gun troop approach one of the many farmsteads in southern Russia. In front of the machine gunner his squad are carrying boxes of ammunition. In 1942 the MG–34 light machine gun was present in every rifle group.

A halftrack with a full complement of crew move along a congested road bound for the Don and Volga Rivers. The troops were unaware of what would greet them once they arrived. They had been given orders to advance east to a city called Stalingrad, which was a major industrial and transportation centre on the west bank of the wide Volga river, the main waterway of inner Russia.

Troops of the 2nd *Panzer* Division move forward across the hot, dry flat steppes. Animal draught has been utilised to tow supplies. On the rear of the single axle trailer some hay is stowed and used as horse feed. Altogether General Paulus's 6th Army contained some 25,000 horses, most of which were used to carry and tow vital supplies to Stalingrad.

A rifle company or *Schützen-Kompanie* march through one of the many fields that covered many hundreds of square miles of the steppe. A rifle company in the summer of 1942 was composed roughly of 190 men. It consisted of three rifle platoons, plus an anti-tank group, which contained seven infantrymen armed with three 7.92mm PzB.39 anti-tank rifles.

Infantrymen march across the steppe purposely spacing themselves apart in order to minimise the threat of aerial attack. The troops are wearing a variety of kit and weapons including the 7.92mm Kar.98k Mauser rifle and ammunition carriers for the MG–34 machine gun. Each rifle company was provided with a heavy machine gun group with two tripod mounted heavy MG–34s.

A Pz.Kpfw.III roars off as the crew clamber through the vehicles hatches. During the early phase of 'Blue' the German offensive gained ground largely because the *Luftwaffe* heavily supported the armoured spearheads and bombed the Red Army as they tried to continuously counterattack.

In action against a suspected enemy position a halftrack halts and takes aim whilst infantry begin to take cover behind the vehicle. This weapon was fed by 20-round magazines. Apart from its unique anti-aircraft capability the flak gun could be used equally, or even better, against light armoured, softskin vehicles, field fortifications and fortified buildings. However, in urbanized fighting these vehicles proved to be highly vulnerable.

A halftrack towing an artillery piece in early July 1942. Out in the open dry steppe the dust that the carriages and vehicles frequently threw into the air could easily be identified from a passing aircraft. Quite regularly whole columns were attacked, but were immediately repulsed by heavy *Luftwaffe* support.

A halftrack motors through a field after a downpour of rain. The halftrack was a vital component to the conduct of operations on the Eastern Front. It not only carried infantry alongside the advancing panzers but it also brought machine guns, mortars, boxes of ammunition and supplies. It also towed anti-tank guns and light anti-aircraft guns, howitzers and pontoon bridge sections to the forefront of the battlefield.

A halftrack towing an artillery piece across the steppe in July 1942. On 17 July the 6th Army issued a communiqué and stated that 'all our units have gained ground in the east according to plan'. Yet progress in many areas was hindered by the lack of maps. A number of units were compelled to advance using nothing more than their compass and reports from aerial reconnaissance.

During 'Operation Blue' grenadiers can be seen entering a deserted village. The grenadier at the end of the column has a MG–34 machine-gun slung over his left shoulder for ease of carriage. A typical machine gun company had a company troop, three heavy machine gun platoons, and a heavy mortar platoon.

Soldier armed with a MP40 machine gun. He can be seen wearing 6x30 binoculars which are secured to a tunic button in order to allow him free movement without them bouncing and swaying.

A dirty-faced German soldier poses for the camera during his march on the Don. During the dry summer months in southern Russia the sand and dust was a constant problem for the soldiers. Not only did the dust and sand particles sift into engine motors and the interior of tanks and other vehicles, but soldiers inhaled it too. Handkerchiefs and other forms of protection were used around the mouth and nose, but this did not prevent the soldier becoming covered with dust.

German infantry on horseback advance along a road and slowly pass a destroyed concrete fortification. By the extent of the damage the enemy position was more than likely knocked out of action by aerial attack.

A German unit temporarily rest during an almost unopposed drive across the steepe. A 10.5cm artillery gun can be just be seen behind the resting horse. The 10.5cm gun was used extensively by German forces in southern Russia during this period. It was primarily the artillery regiments that were given the task of destroying enemy positions and fortified defences and of conducting counter-battery fire prior to an armoured or infantry assault.

A long column of support vehicles and horses towing artillery move steadily along one of the few roads in southern Russia. An average artillery regiment was authorised with some 2,500 troops and 2,274 horses, the latter of which drew over 200 wagons and artillery caissons.

Here a 15cm howitzer is being towed by horses through the mud after a heavy downpour. The 15cm gun was normally broken down into two loads, each drawn by six horses. Although the 15cm howitzer proved a success against enemy targets, by the time 'Operation Blue' was in full swing gun crews found the weapon too heavy. By 1943 only a few of these guns remained in active service and were used mainly in Russia until the end of the war.

Two officers smile for the camera during a pause in 6th Army's advance. Behind the men is a stationary 15cm howitzer being towed by a vehicle. Note the amount of supplies stowed on the gun itself.

A flak gun mounted on the back of a halftrack towing a single axle trailer negotiates an uneven part of terrain. Throughout the war, a number of these vehicles were adapted and were seen mounting various guns. Although both the 2cm and 3.7cm flak gun were used extensively by 6th Army during its drive to the Don, in urbanized fighting its capability would be limited.

Panzergrenadiers from Paulus's 6th Army have hitched a lift on board two Pz.Kpfw.III's. Carrying troops like this was one of the quickest methods to reach the forward edge of the battlefield. When they debussed to go into action, they would help support the armoured spearheads. Although Panzergrenadiers sustained high losses in this way, they could remain very effective, protecting the flanks and keeping open a path for the armour to pour through.

Two Pz.Kpfw.III's advance along a dirt track. *Panzergrenadiers* can be seen riding onboard the tank on the left. *Panzergrenadiers* were considered elite frontline units because of their mobility and the fact that they usually found themselves thrust into battle alongside armoured panzer divisions. These troops were always moved into the thick of battle and provided advancing armour valuable support. Even during the initial stages of the battle of Stalingrad they were able to conduct mobile operations effectively and mop up a bewildered and shocked foe.

A German soldier takes cover in the grass during action in July 1942. Even at this early stage of the offensive it seemed that victory would beckon for the Germans. However, there were still serious concerns that not enough prisoners had been taken and that the 6th Army had got very fearful on the two hundred mile march.

German troops continue their march after destroying a Russian defensive position. By 25 July the 6th Army had been marching continuously for over two weeks and the men were exhausted, but kept pushing forward because they found that in a number of areas resistance was minimal.

A variety of vehicles from the 4th *Panzer* Army have halted on the steppe in late July 1942. During this period the 4th *Panzer* Army were to assume their advance south-eastward along with the 6th Army.

German troops advance towards the town of Manoylin in late July. Five German divisions had attacked the right wing of the Red Army 62nd Army north of Manoylin, whilst other German formations fought the Russian 64th Army north on the Tsimla River. Fighting had gone considerably well for the Germans, despite heavy losses and well defended enemy positions.

German forces begin crossing the Tsimla River after securing the area against Russian soldiers of the 64th Army. By late July the XIV *Panzer* Corps had driven a strong wedge between the Russian 62nd and 64th Armies as it drove for Kalach along the west bank of the Don River.

An artillery regiment march across the steppe bound for the Don River. By early August the Germans were slowly closing in on the city of Stalingrad. General Hoth's 4th *Panzer* Army were steadily advancing from the south and were within forty miles of the city. The 6th Army began preparing to attack areas in front of the river.

A rare opportunity to see German forces preparing to cross the Don River during the 2nd *Panzer* Divisions advance on the Volga in August 1942. Here a halftrack with a full complement of crew are poised to cross the Don.

A divisional column of motor vehicles including a Sd.Kfz.251 halftrack personnel carrier, Horch cross-country cars, as well as civilian vehicles pressed into action, cross a pontoon bridge over the Don.

A Pz.Kpfw.III belonging to the 2nd *Panzer* Division crosses one of the many prefabricated bridges that were erected over marshes boarding the Don River. In the distance other vehicles can also be seen.

A halftrack towing the gun carriage of a 15cm howitzer makes its way towards the Don in August 1942. As the German forces approached the river the Russian 62nd Army ordered its troops to withdraw west of Stalingrad. The situation for the Red Army was now critical.

A Russian artillery piece more than likely belonging to the 62nd Army has been knocked out of action and soldiers of Paulus's 6th Army examine the wreckage. In the first weeks of August alone the 6th Army had killed and captured some 50,000 Soviet troops, but by 18 August with no more than 35 miles from Stalingrad to go, the leading spearheads ran out of fuel again.

Troops make their way forward towards overrun enemy defensive positions near the Don in August. A medical unit are closely following the drive. In front of the ambulance is a Pak35/36 anti-tank gun. Even by 1942 the Pak35/36 was still a popular anti-tank weapon despite it not being very effective against heavier Russian tanks like the T–34.

Russian prisoners from the 62nd Army have been herded together near Kalach. These hapless POWs would soon be marched westward to a grim fate as slave labourers, or worse still, to end their life in a concentration camp like Auschwitz.

A German infantry division's rifle company walk onward towards the Don. At least two MG–34 machine gunners can be seen with their weapons slung over their shoulder. The MG–34 was extensively used by troops on the Eastern front and was used with lethal effect during the battle of Stalingrad.

An excellent display of an infantryman's combat equipment. Note the loaf of bread strapped on top of his canteen. By 1942 many soldiers often had discarded the gas mask canister and carried personal items such as tobacco, letters, and photographs.

Troops trudge forward towards the Don and assist horses as they struggle towing supplies along a typical Russian road. In southern Russia, the all-weather roads had not been constructed to carry the amount and weight of traffic that now used them, and the surfaces began to break up under the strain. Had it been winter, then these roads would have been virtually impassable.

A group of officers observe their advancing units as they make their way towards the western banks of the Don in August 1942. One of the officers observes the movements through a pair of scissor binoculars.

A Pz.Kpfw.III armed with a 5cm gun halts on a road whilst the crew confer with two soldiers. The Pz.Kpfw.III saw widespread service on the Eastern Front and was a formidable adversary to the Soviet T–34 tanks at short ranges.

An 8.8cm flak gun on its limber being towed by a halftrack. Although the 8.8cm flak gun was widely used as an anti-aircraft gun it also possessed a genuine anti-tank capability as well. During the battle of Stalingrad the gun proved a very versatile weapon and continued being used in a dual role until the end of the war.

Due to the terrible lack of maps soldiers invariably had to rely on their compass. Here in this photograph a soldier can be seen obtaining a reading from his compass, flanked by two comrades.

Russian POWs have been captured and escorted to the rear after the 6th Army's drive on the Don in August 1942. These Russian troops probably belong to the 62nd Army, which was suddenly surprised by Paulus's troops on the west bank of the Don.

German troops push forward after repulsing large numbers of enemy units near the Don. The defeat of the Red Army west of Stalingrad caused consternation among the Soviet command, but they did not intend to allow their forces to repeat the same mistake inside Stalin's city.

A halftrack towing a 15cm howitzer belonging to the 6th Army crosses a pontoon bridge during its advance on the Don. A 16-ton pontoon bridge like this was more than capable of allowing the heaviest of German armour to cross a river unhindered.

PART II

Siege of Stalingrad

Bitter Fighting

On 29 August General Hoth's 4th *Panzer* Army launched a new drive from Abganerovo that penetrated both the 64th and 62nd Russian armies. If Paulus could attack from the north as Hoth approached from the south, then the two Russian armies could be encircled and annihilated. On 2 September Paulus dispatched his panzers to make contact with Hoth's force, but by the time they made contact the Russians had already retreated slowly toward Stalingrad. Fighting in the area still raged, and it was made worse by a heavy Luftwaffe attack on the city. German fighters and bombers attacked the city's industrial buildings and tried to prevent the Russians from moving supplies and reinforcements across the river. As the city was pulverized by incessant aerial attacks, on the ground the 6th Army lead corps made a series of attacks into Stalingrad, whilst the 4th *Panzer* Army closed in on its southern outskirts. Fighting their way into the city had been a cruel contest of attrition, but many still believed, even at this stage that victory beckoned. New tactics were employed and the soldiers adopted a simple method of switching their effort to various areas of the city and battering their way at one block for another. Only a few officers saw the danger. The massive Luftwaffe raids had failed to destroy the morale of the Russians, and there were unvoiced concerns that soldiers would soon find themselves stranded in a web of hostile emplacements in the charred remains of a concrete forest that was almost impossible to capture.

What was to follow was a fight equal to the horrors of the battle of Verdun during World War One. However, unlike Verdun where each side rarely saw each other face to face and were killed by long range machine gun fire or blown to bits by artillery, at Stalingrad the battles were fought separately between individuals. Here they fought street by street, where vicious hand-to-hand duels were unleashed among the strewn rubble and burning buildings. Although many of these harden veterans had experienced urbanized fighting before in Russia, nothing could possibly compare to the horrors that they were about to experience.

On 4 September Hoth's forces attacked and battered Russian soldiers of the 64th Army. The very next day the 14th *Panzer* captured Kuporosnoye, a suburb of Stalingrad. As these elite troops of the *Panzergruppe* bull-dozed their way through the city's suburbs, Stalingrad was once more brought under continuous bombardment, as the whole of the 6th Army's artillery smashed and carved a route for Paulus's main attack. On 13 September, two shock forces of the 6th Army converged against the southern half of the city and a bloody battle ensued in the smoke and brick dust. The Russians themselves were hard pressed to defend their meagre positions, but each soldier knew that every foot was precious. Their tanks were only used in small groups of three or four at a time in support of infantry. The Russians would never dare to fire at tanks alone, but let the panzers pass through and be drawn into the field of fire of well dug-in T–34's and anti-tank guns. In this strange wilderness of destruction, panzer crews were very reluctant to take their machines down narrow streets, and always preferred to be accompanied in any attack with teams of flame throwers, so that they could easily burn down buildings which were suspected of being held by the enemy.

Over the following days the soldiers of the 6th Army were slowly drawn into a heavy protracted battle of massive proportions. Along the streets, across the roads, inside houses, and factories, the Russians defended to the last bullet. Even when they found themselves cut off on an island of rubble, there was still a stubborn refusal to surrender. As a consequence of the enemy's dogged determination to hold out to the death German troops would spend whole days clearing a street. Although by late September both sides were exhausted from continuous combat, the Germans were very close to gaining control of the southern part of the city. Back in Germany propaganda slogans were already painting the battle of Stalingrad as 'the greatest battle of attrition the world has ever seen.' Daily published figures showed that the Red Army were being bled to death by 'our heroic warriors.' Yet, 1,500 miles away to the east, the 6th Army was beginning to show signs of frustration and fatigue. The Russians, though now heavily outnumbered were masters in the technique of house-to-house combat. In the

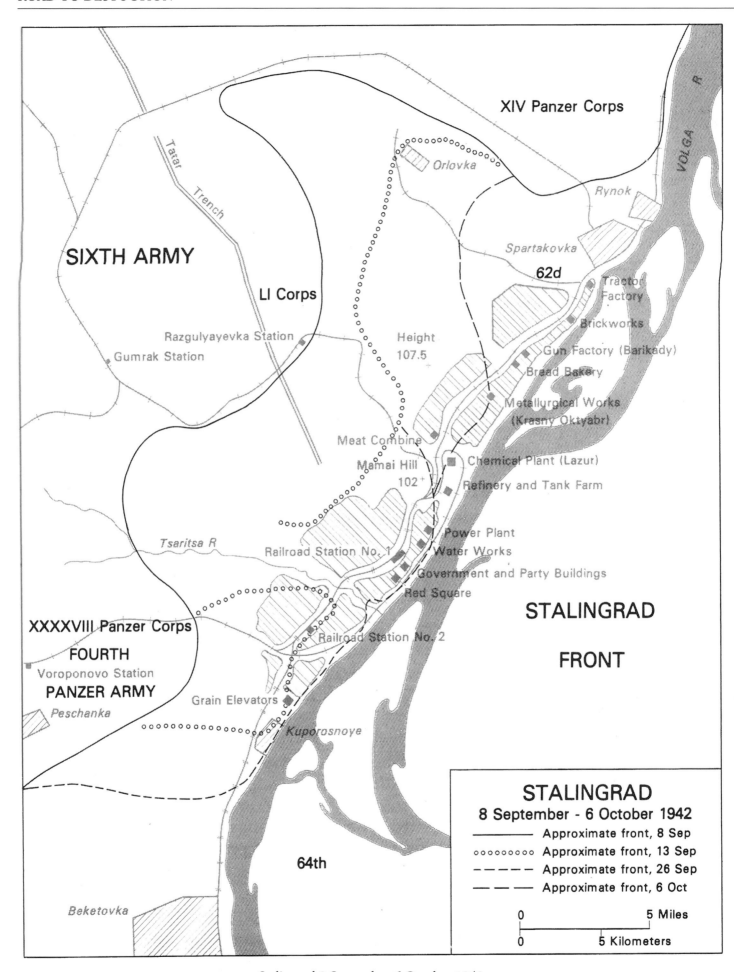

Stalingrad 8 September-6 October 1942
(map appears courtesy of the Center of Military History United States Army, and originally appeared on page 389 of *Moscow to Stalingrad: Decision in the East* by Earl F. Ziemke & Magna E. Bauer, 1987)

burning ruins of the city they had developed the creation of 'killing zones,' where small Russians units were ordered to defend every square yard with machine guns, mortars, grenades, flame throwers and explosive charges. Some street fighting assault squads were armed with spades and knives for silent killing, whilst other more specialised soldiers were assigned to deadly sniper units. In the parklands too, tank crews and soldiers camouflaged their T–34 tanks and anti-tank guns, burying them in rubble or mounds of earth. All channelled approaches were also heavily mined and up to thirty sappers would lay in wait. Some sappers, especially experienced ones, would run out of cover and drop a mine in front of an advancing panzer.

At tremendous cost the Germans inched their way into the furnace of gun fire and shelling. On the northern edge of the city there was a huge grain elevator, and during the third week of September the Germans pounded the building incessantly for three days with artillery, setting the grain on fire. During the night of 20 September the elevator was captured and fighting soon moved to Red square, to a nail factory and the Univermag department store. Over the next few days bitter fighting led to a number of vicious hand-to-hand duels. Losses on both sides were extremely high, but the fighting continued with unabated ferocity.

By 22 September the whole of Stalingrad was a sea of flame and smoke. In the north of the city between Orlovka and Rynok the XVI *Panzer* Division were engaged in heavy fighting. Further south the 71st, 76th,100th, and 295th infantry divisions were engaged in bitter clashes against the 62nd Army along the railway line and the Mechetka River near Gorodishche. South of the city the 24th *Panzer* Division, 29th Motorized Division and the 14th *Panzer* Division made a series of deep penetrations against the 64th Army.

All the troops engaged in the battle were now fighting a bloody, relentless struggle in which buildings became major military objectives. Sometimes the fighting was so fierce that it was often impossible to distinguish friend from foe. Neither side had space to manoeuvre, but the situation favoured the defender, as long as he was willing to shed lots of blood. The Russians were indeed prepared to spill plenty of blood, both their own and that of their hated enemy.

Into the Cauldron

During the last week of September 1942 with the 6th Army still struggling to capture Stalingrad, the Rumanian 3rd Army were ordered to take over Paulus's front west of the Don. These Romanian forces were regarded by the Germans as the most important allied formation to be given the task of protecting the flanks of the 6th Army, but they were quite unsuited to independent front-line operations against the might of the Red Army. Not only were they ill-equipped, short of rations and winter clothing, they were not up to strength, despite draughting some 2,000 civilian convicts sentenced for rape, looting and murder. Germans of all ranks that came into contact with their Romanian allies were not only surprised at the way their officers treated their men, but the way they fought and defended on the battlefield. In late September the Germans were eventually given a demonstration of their ability against the Russians. On the 28th the Rumanians were immediately repulsed on the 6th Army's right flank against what the Germans considered were relatively weak enemy units. As the Rumanian forces retreated Hoth's 4th *Panzer* Army was immediately wheeled up to prevent the rout, and by the end of the month had stabilized the front once more.

Inside the city intensive fighting continued as General Zhukov made plans to bring catastrophe to the Germans. On 6 October Paulus temporarily suspended further attacks into the city. His infantry strength had been badly depleted. In the first six weeks since his army moved from the Don, 7,700 soldiers had been killed and 31,000 wounded. Ten percent of his army was destroyed. In one division alone the infantry battalions had an average of 3 officers, 11 noncommissioned officers, and only 62 men. The ammunition too was dwindling and they were in desperate need of resupply. In September alone the army had fired off more than 25 million rounds of small arms ammunition, half a million anti-tank rounds, and three quarters of a million artillery shells. Paulus required at least 650 tons of supplies a day to survive. To make matters worse the *Führer* demanded that Stalingrad be captured by 15 October. However, it was not until 14 October after receiving five special pioneer battalions, an infantry division from the 6th Army's flank, and a panzer division from the 4 *Panzer* Army, that Paulus was prepared to renew his attack. The attack was billed as 'the final offensive,' but in reality even Paulus knew he was unable to capture the city by the 15th. Instead, his men pushed forward into the city and resumed their relentless war which was dubbed the *Rattenkrieg* (rat war). Here amidst death and carnage they began living and fighting as rats. Through the rubble, twisted steel of factories, shattered and burnt out wooden houses, cells, sewers, trenches and holes, they fought and tried to survive. In order to try and reduce the casualties halftracks carrying grenadiers were utilized, but because they were open-topped and lightly armoured the vehicles were little use inside the city and they were highly vulnerable to close attack. *Panzer* and assault guns too like the

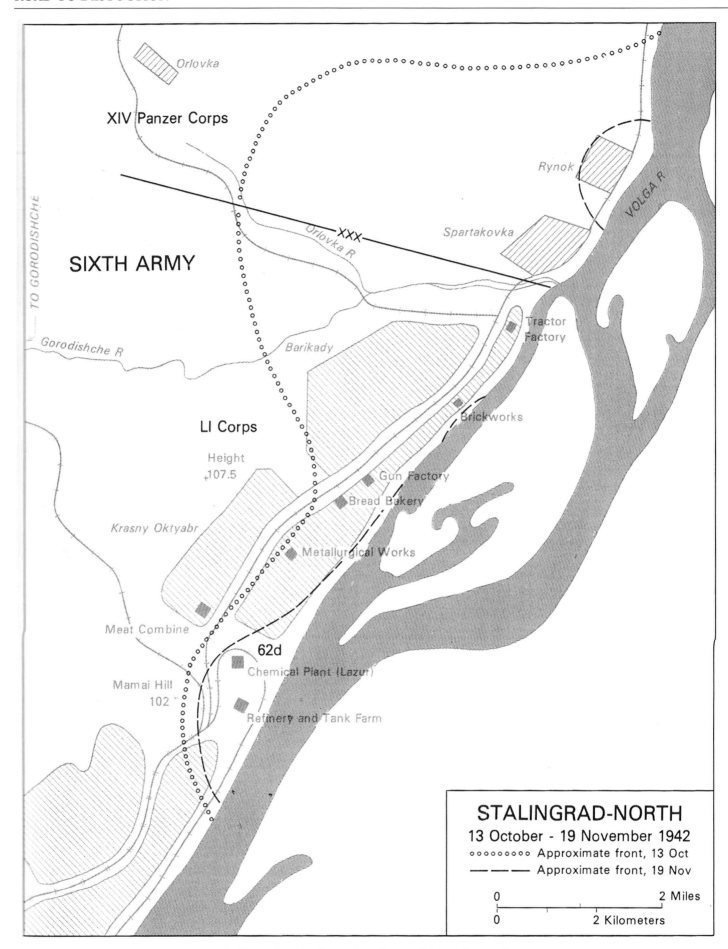

Stalingrad – North, 13 October-19 November 1942
(map appears courtesy of the Center of Military History United States Army, and originally appeared on page 461 of *Moscow to Stalingrad: Decision in the East* by Earl F. Ziemke & Magna E. Bauer, 1987)

Pz.Kpfw.III, Pz.Kpfw.IV, StuG.III, and Marder, were also knocked out of action. The crews that were fortunate enough to survive soon became infantrymen, frequently exchanging their black uniforms for field grey from the dead. Every man that could be mustered for the 'final battle' was put into the line. Many pioneers, trained to support the main assaults, were ordered to serve as infantry. Luftwaffe ground personnel and Flak troops fought as infantrymen as well along with police troops.

During the 14 October Paulus sent five divisions against the Barrikady and tractor factory. By midnight after heavy sustained fighting they had completely surrounded the tractor plant. Losses, however, had been very heavy and during the course of the night some 3,500 wounded were reported. Hour after hour further fighting raged with uncompromising harshness as the German 389th Infantry Division moved deeper into the city. To these dirty and dishevelled soldiers, the thought of withdrawing now after shedding so much blood seemed unthinkable. Instead, they had to push on and endure the battle with a terrible prospect of being killed, wounded, or worst still, captured by the Russians. Behind the lines the German war cemeteries were growing every day. Commanders were alarmed seeing for themselves badly mauled regiments returning to the lines with heavy casualties, and suffering low morale. To them the battle depended on nerves of steel as much as resources. But even resources and willpower alone could not avert the terrible circumstances, and the fact that their enemy were now concentrating over half a million infantry, nearly 1,000 new T–34's, 230 regiments of field artillery, and over 100 regiments of *Katyushas* rocket mortars into the great battle ever fought thus far on the Eastern Front.

While Zhukov's armies moved into position, the Germans tried their best to gather up enough strength for further fighting in the rubble and burning remains of the doomed city. The difficulties were made worse by the increasing reports of larger Russian formations bearing down on Stalingrad. The situation deteriorated further when Hungarian, Italian, and Rumanian allied forces were beginning to show signs of crumbling. These ill-equipped, badly trained soldiers had been sent to help bolster their German allies. But after weeks of constant fighting against overwhelming enemy forces the soldiers began deserting. For days many of them sat huddled in stinking rat infested trenches, clinging to life under a constant barrage of unparalleled intensity. As they deserted their cratered lines with their backs to Stalingrad, they followed a path of unspeakable hell. Mile after mile, hundreds upon hundreds of them were either killed by tank fire, shelling, or aerial attack. Those that were fortunate enough to escape the slaughter were normally lightly clothed, and with no protection from the cold they simply froze to death on the steppe.

Whilst Germany's allies tried to stay alive around Stalingrad, inside the city itself the fighting had intensified. By 23 October the Germans held the tractor factory and most of the Barrikady factory, whilst the Red Army held positions inside the Red October Factory. Two days later the Germans captured the centre of Spartakovka, and the 6th Army nearly reached the Volga. The next day they were pushed back with serious losses. But undeterred by the growing casualties the German 100th Infantry Division used artillery to blast its way through Russian positions, where it soon managed to be within firing range of the last remaining Russian ferry landing on the western shore. German squads from the 100th Division were sure that victory was imminent. The Germans now held nine-tenths of the city, and the last remaining part was under merciless fire. The Russians still held the last few remaining buildings along the Volga, which stretched for about six miles, but only a few hundred yards wide. The situation for the Red Army in Stalingrad was dire, yet they were still fanatically holding-out.

During the last days of October ceaseless fighting continued, but Paulus's men were exhausted and low on supplies. By the 30th their attacks had grown weaker allowing Russian soldiers of the 62nd Army to build-up strength. The cost had been terrible, but now more reinforcements and supplies were on the way. The Red Army's grim determination to holdout at all costs had proven vital for the survival of its men fighting in the ruins of Stalingrad. With the onset of winter fast approaching they were sure the tide would turn in their favour.

Operation Uranus

Whilst fighting continued inside Stalingrad on the Don River the German XI Corps was given the task of supporting the left flank of the 6th Army. Here Russian forces of the 65th Army continued to harass German and allied positions. The Romanian 3rd Army, the Italian 8th Army and the Hungarian 2nd Amy were bearing the brunt of many of the attacks. In order to support the hard pressed allies the XLVII *Panzer* Corps, which included one German and one Romanian panzer division was hurriedly dispatched. But because many of the tanks in the division had been lying for weeks camouflaged on the Don Front, mice had eaten into the tanks vital electrical wiring system. As a consequence only 39 out of the 104 panzers were able to move, whilst another 34 later developed electrical problems and broke down. Though a number of the tanks were later repaired and hastily sent to support the XI. Corps, many of the vehicles, especially in the Romanian 1st Armoured Division were Czech

Pz.Kpfw.35 (t)'s and Pz.Kpfw.38 (t)'s. These models were enormously inferior to the Russian tanks and many of them were knocked out of action during their first contact.

During this period the winter suddenly arrived in early November. Although the Germans were being supplied with winter clothing from a supply chain via Kharkov, some four hundred miles away to the west, the horrors of the last Russian winter was still impregnated in every soldiers mind. Even as the first snow showers settled along the front on the Don fighting continued. On 2 November the Russians threw several new brigades across the Don to the Serafimovich bridgehead. Two days later the 6th *Panzer* Division and two infantry divisions were immediately transferred from the English Channel coast to Army Group B, where they were to be employed as reserve forces behind the Italian 8th and Rumanian 3rd Armies. It was clear from aerial photos that the Russians were slowly building-up their forces around Stalingrad and preparing for a major offensive. German intelligence deduced that Russian forces along the Don were preparing to attack the Rumanian 3rd Army with the sole objective of cutting the railroad to Stalingrad and threatening troops of the 6th Army. It now appeared that the Stalingrad offensive was now moving into a new stage in the Soviet conduct of operations. Most significant was Russian independent armoured formations mixed with infantry had broken through to the German rear and were exploiting weak Rumanian defensive positions.

Early on the morning of the 19 November these Rumanian defences were finally put to the test by a massive Russian offensive, code named 'Operation Uranus'. For miles, hundreds of tanks, artillery, and thousands of men burst onto the German line 100-miles north-west of Stalingrad, at the point where Rumanian troops made up much of the defensive formations. At the same time another thrust from the south was made to help catch the German forces in a gigantic encirclement. Inferior in military tactics to the ordinary Russian infantry, Rumanian soldiers were bombed and blasted by lines of rocket launchers, waves of soldiers, and spearheads of tank. Within hours of the first punishing strikes, the rear-echelon units were fleeing for their lives in the snow as Russian tanks broke through the main line. The Rumanian 1st Armoured Division was ordered up from reserve, but ran head-on into a Russian advance of the 5th Tank Army, and was subsequently annihilated. General Paulus could do nothing to help his Rumanian allies. Instead, he had to listen to disturbing reports of how the Rumanian 4th Army, which was defending south of the city, were chased by Russian tanks, assaulted on the flanks by infantry and horse cavalry. Slowly they were destroyed piece by piece by long-range rocket and artillery barrages, while at the same time struggling through deep snow in terrible arctic temperatures.

On the third day of 'Operation Uranus', the brave Rumanian commander Major-General Lascar, who had witnessed the death of thousands of his comrades in one of the fiercest battles on the Eastern Front, was awarded by Hitler the Oak Leaves to the Knight's Cross, Germany's highest medal. He was the first non-German to be honoured, but his decoration did nothing to prevent the complete collapse of the Rumanians on both flanks of the 6th Army. By 24 November, more than 30,000 Rumanian soldiers had capitulated. The almost total destruction of the Rumanian army meant that Paulus's troops were now cut off and surrounded. Stalingrad now had a perimeter of 150-miles held grimly by 19 German divisions, the Rumanian 20th and 1st Cavalry divisions, the Croatian 369th Regiment, including thousands of Axis personnel.

On the Don to the right of the Italians, Rumanian troops managed to hold positions along the Chir River by frantically gathering stragglers to form a barrier against the increasingly strong Russian forces. But the situation on these Russian steppes was far more serious than ever before. As the death toll rose daily and further setback intensified, the Germans blamed their Rumanian allies for the disaster that was looming at Stalingrad. The Rumanians, however, blamed their government for having deployed them so far into Russia, when their original plan had been only to liberate Bessarabia and Northern Bukovina.

With Germany's allies struggling for survival the Red Army were slowly closing their mighty jaws around Stalingrad. German troops were virtually swamped in a sea of death and fire. As Russian soldiers surged forward, the tanks and artillery remained in front of them, carpeting the area a head with shells, rockets and gun fire. In the ranks were well seasoned troops that had fought for months defending their homeland. They had lived for this moment of revenge. Now they were determined to win at all costs, even if it meant sacrificing thousands in the process.

Over the next few days the Germans struggled against overwhelming superiority. Zhukov had moved some 134 divisions swept over the Don. Masses of tanks and infantry then spewed across the frozen steppe, whilst hard pressed German forces frenetically tried to contain them. As the German situation further deteriorated the 4th *Panzer* Army, including two Romanian corps remnants, was designated Army Group Hoth. Day and night Hoth's *Gruppe* fought desperately to try and stem the advance of the Russian units that were beginning to encircle Stalingrad. Both sides of the Don, east and west, and across the steppe towards the smouldering city of Stalingrad bore the unmistakable signs of battle. For miles the wreckage of broken divisions littered the area. But these were not Russian divisions; they were disorganized German and Rumanian units that had frantically clawed their way out of the clutches of the Russian tanks. Over fifty miles north and thirty south the whole German and Rumanian front was broken up and flattened. Even the XLVIII *Panzer* Corps had been simply brushed aside by the Russian onslaught. With total dissolution of their foreign allies, Paulus saw his 6th Army as the only fighting formation capable of inflicting serious damage against their dreaded enemy. But his enemy had already concentrated a massive iron ring around his army. Along the western and southern flanks of the pocket, more than 1,000 Russian anti-tank guns alone had been positioned running from Vertyachiy, bending eastward from below Marinovka to join the Volga south of Stalingrad. This Russian employment of firepower was the first steps towards the annihilation of more than a quarter of a million German soldiers. If a break out in Stalingrad was ever to succeed, Paulus had to act now before the turning point on the Eastern Front was forged forever.

Entombment

During the night of 23 November battle-fatigued divisions of Paulus's 6th Army had become trapped in and around the ruins of Stalingrad. To the north and east of what became known to the men as the cauldron or *Kessel*, the soldiers constructed natural shelters out of the merciless elements. But out on the southern and western parts of the *Kessel*, fatigued units found themselves dug-in across the frozen bare open steppe living in trenches against the bitter cold, howling wind, and driving snow. In all, across this huge expanse of land some 265,000 men including some 12,000 Rumanians, 1,800 guns, over 100 tanks, 10,000 assorted vehicles with some 21,000 horses, were en-tombed and exposed daily to the full blast of Russian artillery and rocket fire. Inside Stalingrad itself, among the wasteland of destruction, Russian soldiers used their masterly tactics in urbanized killing by beginning round the clock counter-attacks. What followed were countless murderous confrontations between small groups of German soldiers that were less suited for urbanized warfare than that of their dreaded foe. Not only were the Germans at-tempting too much, but they were relying on their *Führer* who had decided to ignore the perils of being drawn into a major confrontation inside the streets of a large city. Paulus had become seriously concerned about the deteriorat-ing situation and hoped that Field Marshal von Manstein, who had just assumed command of Army Group Don, would do everything possible to relieve his beleaguered 6th Army trapped in and around Stalingrad.

On 24 November as Manstein assembled the 6th, 17th and 23rd *Panzer* divisions, and the 16th Motorized Divi-sions for a relief attempt on Stalingrad, General Wolfram Freiherr von Richthofen's *Luftwaffe IV* was given the responsibility for supplying the 6th Army by means of an arduous airlift. Not only was Richthofen faced with an impossible situation of delivering 500-tons of supplies per day, which was the tonnage necessary to sustain Paulus's men, but most of his aircrew were young and inexperienced. The long dangerous approach to the *Kessel* and the return flights over an enemy territory infested with swarms of Russian fighters and anti-tank guns was suicidal. To make matters worse morale among the aircrews were badly affected at the sight of the doomed, battle weary and half-starved German forces trapped in the entombed city. To abandon thousands of wounded, frostbitten and dying comrades behind in the snow because there was not sufficient space available to fly them out, also put a heavy strain on them psychologically.

In total *Luftwaffe IV* had forty-seven Ju–52's available to fly in supplies to maintain 6th Army's fighting strength. When the first sorties left their airfields west of the Don on 24 November, twenty-two were shot down, many of which never even reached the city. The following day another nine were lost to heavy anti-flak batteries along the Don and enemy fighter attacks. As a consequence only 75-tons had been supplied, instead of the 300-tons initially earmarked for the 6th Army. Paulus had now become increasingly desperate, but he still pinned all his hopes on the *Luftwaffe* and Manstein's forces.

By 28 November the Russian encirclement of Stalingrad was finally completed. The Red Army had won a great victory in the bend of the Don and had cast out a gigantic envelopment around more than a quarter of a million German troops between the Don and Stalingrad. Inside the city the physical condition of the once glorious 6th Army that had steamrolled across into Russia seventeen-months earlier were now a force fighting for survival. Inadequate diet, the bitter inescapable cold and dwindling mail from loved ones at home, began to rapidly cause an acute decline in morale. Paulus was totally aware that if his army was to be saved, it would have to be done soon. Richthofen suggested that the 6th Army be allowed to break out, but Hitler flatly rejected the proposal out of hand. Paulus was to stand fast and not to move back one yard. Hitler made it clear that he would be supplied by the *Luftwaffe* and a relief operation by Manstein would ensure a successful outcome. Richthofen knew that the aircraft employed were insufficient to decisively improve the air supply. His remaining aircraft and those newly delivered to airfields in the south had to cross heavily defended enemy held-territory. Every pilot had to fly through contested air space, without adequate ground support, and never knowing if they would ever reach their target successfully.

On 29 November, thirty-eight Ju–52's and twenty-one He–111's left their airfields west of the Don bound for the pocket. Of those, twelve JU52's and thirteen He–111's landed inside the pocket. The following day thirty Ju–52's and thirty-six He–111's successfully landed. This was a remarkable achievement, but the operation had to be maintained on a daily basis if the besieged troops were to survive. However, the Russians were determined to stem the Stalingrad airlift. On 1 December the 8th and 16th Red Army Air Forces concentrated their fleet of fighters against the German bombers as they attempted to fly their vital supplies to Pitomnik inside the circle. Within two days the Russians had shot down twenty-eight aircraft, most of which were the lumbering Ju–52's.

Whilst Richthofen's pilots continued bravely flying into the pocket against overwhelming enemy superiority, Army Group Don began preparations for 'Operation Winter Storm', the relief of the 6th Army. The undertaking was daring for the Russians were on every side of the *Kessel*. In the north, not far from the banks of the Volga, were the 16th and 24th *Panzer* divisions. Fighting in the northwest were the 44th, 76th, and 384th divisions. In the west were remnants of the 376th Division, 3rd Motorized Division, 160th Motorized Division, and the 113th Infantry Division. In the south were 297th and 371st Infantry divisions and the 29th Motorized Division. In reserve but trapped inside the *Kessel* were the 14th *Panzer* Division and the 9th Flak Division, two Rumanian divisions, and one regiment of Croatians. In the east, fighting inside the city itself were the shattered and exhausted divisions of the 71st, 79th, 100th, 295th, 305th, and 389th. The men had come very close to winning the battle in October, but now five weeks later in this cratered shell of a city they were fighting with almost primeval fury to survive. For many of the soldiers there seemed no end to the continuous battles and bloodshed. Their only salvation seemed to be a pending relief expedition to Stalingrad by Army Group Don.

In early December Paulus was given encouraging news that Manstein was finally putting together a task force to march on the city. But unknown to the General much of the mixed units that were formed had received hardly any infantry training and knew virtually nothing about urbanized warfare. They also had insufficient supplies of heavy artillery, anti-tank and flak guns. Nevertheless, Manstein was a brilliant commander and was able to scrape-up additional forces including the 11th and 6th *Panzer* divisions, and the 62nd and 294th Infantry, and a *Luftwaffe* division and a *Gebirgsjäger* division. This new force under the command of General Karl Hollidt and named the 'Hollidt Force', were assigned to support the 4th *Panzer* Army's LVII *Panzer* Corps drive north eastward from the vicinity of Kotelnikovo toward Stalingrad. Other supporting forces along the Chir would then to attack out of the Chir bridgehead, whilst the 6th Army attempted to breakout to the south.

The plans to relieve Paulus's troops in Stalingrad seemed impressive, but as each day ominously dragged on towards Manstein's launch date, 'Operation Winter Storm' grew less promising. But if Manstein was to fail in his relief effort, then it was certain that the 6th Army would perish in the fiery cauldron of Stalingrad.

A German soldier in a corn field. Attached to his steel helmet is foliage which is being held in place by rubber rings. Individuals sometimes utilized various other bits of materials around their helmets to keep foliage in place, including elasticated rings, cloth rags, and chicken wire mesh.

Here MG–34 gunners are using their machine gun in an anti-aircraft role against low flying enemy targets. The MG–34 was a very effective weapon and on its sustained mount in an AA role it was more than capable of damaging, or even bringing down, an aircraft.

A heavily camouflaged Sd.Kfz.251 halftrack has halted behind a building, using it as cover whilst a *Panzergrenadier* can be seen moving forward into action. The performance of the *Panzergrenadiers* in battle was mainly attributed to the Sd.Kfz.251 transporting these infantry units on to the battlefield. However, in Stalingrad these vehicles were prone to attack and many were lost in the urbanized fighting.

A MG–34 machine gun crew sited among a ruined Russian defensive position. A well sighted, well hidden and well-supplied MG–34 could hold up an entire attacking regiment. This machine gun is perfectly sighted, and could inflict heavy losses on an enemy advance. Inside Stalingrad the MG–34 would prove its worth time and time again.

An infantry observes Russian positions along the Don which have come under heavy ground and aerial attack. The soldier is wearing the regulation army-issue camouflage helmet cover and is armed with the standard German Karabiner 98K rifle. The weapon weighed some 4kg (8.8Ib) and had a magazine capacity of five rounds.

An Sd.Kfz.251 halftrack approaches a knocked out Russian T–34 tank. The halftrack is armed with a MG–34 machine gun and fitted with a protective shield. The shield however only offered the gunners minimal protection, especially whilst heavily embroiled in street fighting like Stalingrad.

Soldiers with their MG–34 machine gun in a light machine gun role used with a bipod. Note the weapons assault drum which contained a 50-rounds belt. With entrenching tool and shovel the feeder appears to be preparing the machine gun nest by moving earth in order to camouflage their position.

One of the many defensive positions built on the Don in August 1942. Whilst the Germans were busily digging in along the Don, further east some 200,000 defenders, soldiers and civilians, frantically dug anti-tank ditches and trenches, built pillboxes and other defensive positions, as they prepared for the German onslaught on Stalingrad.

A rare opportunity to see a variety of vehicles preparing to cross the Don River in August 1942. Among the vehicles are halftrack personnel carriers, Opel 'Blitz' trucks, and a number of other vehicles.

A divisional pioneer battalion is busily completing the construction of a bridge across the Don in August 1942. A halftrack personnel carrier can be seen limbered to a trailer hauling wood and other pieces of bridging equipment.

A soldier scours a field ahead for any signs of enemy movement. In the quietest sectors of the front German trenches such as this one were manned by only a few troops. By the winter of 1942 many soldiers were compelled to use these trenches as living quarters, which were totally inadequate.

On 21 August XIV *Panzer* Corps broke out and in three days it had spearheaded through to the Volga north of Stalingrad. In order for it to keep a toe hold on the river, the corps had to break contact with the army and form a hedgehog. Here in this photograph a troop leader scans for enemy armour next to a Pak 35/36 anti-tank gun.

On 23 August advanced elements of the 6th Army reach the Volga just north of Stalingrad and managed to capture a 5 mile strip along the river. Here in this photograph troops move forward in to action against suspected enemy troop

Infantrymen approaching the Volga on 23 August. The men are examining an empty Russian dugout, which was part of the cities outer defences. During their drive east many Soviet troops evacuated their defensive positions in front of the Volga and withdrew into the city.

As German armour and motorized infantry push forward they attack and destroy anything that moves. Here a Russian tank has been knocked out of action and is on fire. By the morning of 24 August it was reported by a Russian pilot that two columns each of 100 German tanks followed by motorized infantry, were bearing down on Stalingrad with heavy air support.

These infantrymen have dug rifle firing positions along an edge of a field not far from the Volga. Dug in positions like this were invariably common and helped reduce the number of fatalities from low flying Russian aircraft.

A machine gun team of the 6th Army prepare to move forward during intensive fighting on the outskirts of Stalingrad. Soviet pressure was already causing the Germans problems north of the city. But by 1 September units of the 6th Army had successfully reached the suburbs of the city following fierce fighting.

Troops pull a Pak 35/36 anti-tank gun through a field past a bomb crater towards the Volga. On 3 September both the 6th Army and 4th *Panzer* Army linked up and the Germans now began surrounding Stalingrad on the west side of the Volga.

A MG–34 machine gunner and his squad move along a railway line near Gumrak in early September. Russian rolling stock stands idle after the railway line travelling into the city was destroyed. By this period the city was already a mass of ruins and fires could be seen for miles.

A machine gun team prepared to go into action in the western suburbs of Stalingrad. By the morning of 5 September troops along with panzers had broken through strongly defended enemy positions and captured the heights overlooking the city just west of Stalingrad.

Two artillery men carefully prepare an artillery shell for firing against targets on the Volga. Throughout the battle of Stalingrad more than 35,000 runs were made by the Russians across the Volga in a desperate attempt to supply their troops and

With a pair of binoculars a soldier surveys the terrain ahead and tries to deduce the location of the enemy. His steel helmet is well camouflaged with foliage. However in Stalingrad, among the ruined buildings troops often smeared their helmets with brick dust and dirt.

Using a pair of scissor binoculars from a dug-out position on the Volga a soldier observes enemy movement. By 14 September Paulus's 6th Army had forced the Russian 62nd Army back into the industrial areas of Stalingrad along the west bank of the Volga. Here troops are preparing to attack Russian forces on the western shores of the river.

A German soldier poses for the camera inside a freshly prepared dug out during the initial stages of the battle of Stalingrad. Fighting in and around the city was now almost continuous and although the 6th Army reported to have made some successful breakthroughs the Russians were still fighting desperately and not giving themselves up.

A typical German defensive position on the Volga in September 1942. Although unable to sustain heavy systematic bombardments from the enemy these positions offered the men some degree of shelter from the rain and later the snow. Many hundreds of these dug outs were built between the Don and Volga rivers during the battle.

Not far from the river's edge and supported by a MG–34 machine gun on its sustained fire-mount, infantry men are poised before resuming their attack into Stalingrad. By the appearance of their uniforms the soldiers appear to be relatively fresh.

Standing in his trench a MG–34 machine-gunner scours the terrain ahead. The position is defended by a Pak35/36 anti-tank gun and a MG–34 machine gun. A trench like this was quite capable of causing some serious damage to its opponent, even though the Pak35/36 had become inadequate for operational needs in the face of growing armoured opposition.

Soldiers are about to move forward once again into action. During mid-September the Germans assaulted enemy positions numerous times each day, but the Soviets would repeatedly respond with fierce counterattacks, often causing unprecedented amounts of casualties.

Landser of the 267th Infantry Regiment of the 94th Infantry Division use a deserted Russian farmstead as a defensive position not far from the Volga. A Pak35/36 can be seen in action. During the battle of Stalingrad the Pak35/36 was used extensively against both armoured and infantry targets.

On the Volga troops can be seen erecting one of the many shelters that were built along the river. When the temperature severely dropped at the end of October, these shelters were a lifeline for the soldiers. Many troops that did not have adequate shelter often froze to death on the steppe during the battle.

A German position on the steppe between the Don and Volga in September 1942. Troops have made great use of the local terrain and built shelters into the sides of the gully. Tents and other shelters have also been erected. A 15cm howitzer can be seen in the background in an elevated position.

Two newly decorated signal operators jot down messages that they have received. The soldier on the right who holds the rank of *Gefreiter* wears on his upper left sleeve a signal operators badge that consisted of a lightening 'Blitz' in yellow on a dark blue-green oval background.

A MG–34 machine gun troop rest on the slope of a hill during a lull in fighting near the Volga. It is evident that the troops have used their entrenching tools to dig in and help protect themselves from enemy fire.

Moving forward through the outskirts of Stalingrad is a column of soldiers escorted by a single axle twin machine gun wagon. The wagon is being towed by what appears to be a halftrack. Once embroiled in heavy infantry fighting the MG–34's could be dismounted and fired from their integral bipods or from the two *Lafette* 34 mount tripods, which were carried in the limber or a supporting vehicle.

Keeping low a group of infantry move forward using a slit trench as cover as they attempt to advance through the outskirts of the city. German infantry frequently adopted a simple method of switching their efforts of assault between various areas in the city and battering from one block to another.

As German forces made a series of penetrating assaults into Stalingrad out on the Steppe intensive Russian aerial activity bombed and blasted German positions. Here in this photograph German troops move forward after Russian aircraft attacked their forward positions. The Volga and the city are obscured by the black smoke.

A much needed respite, troops rest inside a dug out during a pause in the fighting on the steppe. By the winter much of the steppe was impossible to dig in with infantry hand tools because of the hard frozen ground. Often high explosive charges were employed to blast holes in the earth in order to give the troops some kind of protection against the elements and enemy

On the outskirts of Stalingrad Russian worker houses burn furiously following heavy fighting. The workers buildings, consisting of flats and single storey wooden houses, were heavily defended by Red Army troops as strong points.

Two radio operators can be seen inside a shelter on the steppe. The soldiers appear to have been here for some reasonable time as two *Zeltbahn* capes have been used as a tent. There were a number of standard designs for constructing *Zeltbahn* tents and some of them could house four, eight and even sixteen men. These *Zeltbahn* tents were ideal rainproof shelters and were used extensively throughout the war, but they were not designed for front line use. They were, however, used for covering the doorways of bunkers.

Out on the steppe in October 1942 and a howitzer crew pose for the camera during a pause in the fighting. The power of these heavy field guns could hurl their destructive charge nearly 9 miles into the enemy lines.

Two photographs taken in September showing flak crews during a lull in the fighting on the steppe. Both the 2cm and 3.7cm flak gun became the primary light anti-aircraft gun used by the Germans out on the steppe in 1942. However, due to the recurring appearance of heavier enemy armour it compelled flak crews to divert their attention from the air and support their own infantry and armour on the ground in an anti-tank role. Both weapons are mounted on its cruciform platform and had an effective firing rate of 120–280 rounds per minute.

A halftrack towing a 15cm howitzer steadily crosses a makeshift bridge over the numerous marshes boarding the Don River. The 15cm field gun was designed to attack targets deep in the enemy's rear. This included command posts, reserve units, assembly areas, and logistics facilities.

A German outpost during the fight into the city. Two soldiers in a slit trench are armed with a MG–34 machine gun. The weapon is mounted on a *Lafette* 34 mount tripod and is being used against low flying enemy aircraft.

Soldiers are sheltering among bomb craters as they pause in their advance into Stalingrad. By early October both the German attackers and Russian defenders had almost reached stalemate, with neither side able to effectively deliver the decisive blow.

German infantry hastily make their way along a captured Soviet trench near Orlovka. In early October the Germans unleashed a large scale assault into Stalingrad and attacked the Orlovka salient that projected westwards from the northern suburb of Rynok.

71

One of the many workers houses that were destroyed during the battle of Stalingrad. Two soldiers pass the burning building. The leading infantryman is armed with a MG–34 machine gun.

Whilst taking respite beside one of the very few wooden buildings left unscathed by the battle a company commander speaks to his men. By early October the 6th Army had suffered huge casualties. Since 13 September it had incurred more than 40,000 killed and wounded. October was ultimately the most important month for the survival of the 6th Army. If it failed to take the city it would be doomed.

Soldiers approach the Stalingrad suburbs, passing workers flats and houses. In the distance smoke rises from the burning fuel tanks close to the Volga. Night and day the oil-storage tanks burned. Soldiers complained of the choking fumes which made breathing sometimes very difficult.

A StuG.III assault gun moves forward on the out skirts of Stalingrad whilst German infantry follow closely behind. The StuG.III was primarily to provide attacking infantry with adequate fire support. Although it had proven its worth on the Eastern Front the vehicle did not have a turret and had limited traverse. As a consequence many of the assault guns were unable to provide sufficient infantry support whilst fighting inside the city.

A halftrack with a mounted flak gun fires at an enemy position near the banks of the Volga. Though these vehicles rarely saw action inside the city, they were used widely on the steppe against both ground and aerial targets. With the folded down sides the gun was very adaptable and could traverse 360 degrees, making it a very lethal weapon of war.

Two infantrymen hide behind a Pak gun in front of the Volga in October 1942. The soldier on the right is armed with an MP–40 submachine gun. The gun was a very effective weapon and used extensively during the battle of Stalingrad. However, troops soon learned whilst fighting in the city that the MP–40 was prone to debris and brick dust, and the soldier often had to give the magazine a slap to restore its operation.

German soldiers of the 100th Infantry Division have utilized a destroyed wooden building and turned it into a makeshift shelter between Gorodishche and the tractor factory. By early October the Germans were concentrating tanks and infantry in the gullies around the tractor factory and Barrikady factory.

As the 100th Infantry Division fights its way through towards the tractor factory on 4 October the Germans overrun a number of Russian defensive positions. Here in this photograph a German soldier moves stealthily through a captured trench and climbs over the bodies of dead Russian soldiers.

German infantry push forward into the city and use a destroyed building as temporary cover before resuming their assault. Many of the buildings in Stalingrad offered the soldiers relatively good cover and provided better protection from small arms rounds and

A soldier stands casually at the entrance of his shelter which has been called the 'Savoy Hotel'. Behind the man the two signs read 'Wolga Bar' and offers a teatime dance at 5. These bunkers were known by the troops as small houses.

A German soldier hastily makes a dash through the wasteland of the northern suburbs. Russian sniper fire was a frequent problem in Stalingrad and many troops preferred not to take chances by staying out in the open for any appreciable length of

A *Panzergrenadier* uses a Pz.Kpfw.III as cover whilst he scours the destroyed street using a pair of binoculars trying to locate hiding enemy soldiers. By October the Russians were now fighting in small, heavily armed storm groups in order to carry out lightning attacks on buildings and strong points.

One common method of carrying machine gun ammunition boxes was the use of a rifle sling placed around the back of the neck and over the shoulders. The boxes would then be attached either side and given a balanced load. Carrying ammunition like this allowed the soldier to move more freely whilst on the move, and with another 50-round belt draped around his neck it gave his machine gun troop more staying power on the battlefield.

A mortar crewman is seen carrying a 10-round ammunition case for a 5cm I.GrW36 light mortar. The I.Gr.W36 fired a small 0.9kg (1.96Ib) charge to a maximum range of 500m (547yds). Though this mortar was used widely in Stalingrad production of the weapon had in fact been phased out in 1942 due to it lacking sufficient punch.

A MG–34 machine gunner moves forward into action. In Stalingrad the Germans developed effective defensive tactics and techniques designed around the formidable MG–34 and MG–42 machine gun. In a number of battles that raged throughout the city the weapon had considerable staying power.

Infantry rest behind an Sd.Kfz.251 personnel carrier. In Stalingrad the Sd.Kfz.251 halftrack was used to carry men into the city. The vehicle possessed rear doors and the crew compartment was left open so that the soldiers could hastily disembark over the sides and take up primary positions in order to try and mop up a bewildered enemy. However, quite often the halftrack was prone to attack by both small arms and machine gun fire. Bottles of Molotov cocktails too were thrown into the open compartment setting fire to the soldiers inside.

From a position on the outskirts of the city a mortar crew prepares to use their weapon. In Stalingrad the mortar was a valuable high explosive weapon capable beyond the ranges of rifles or hand grenades. However, it lacked accuracy and normally for every ten projectiles fired only one hit the target.

Here Russian troops outside the city push a 45mm (1.77in) Model 1932 L/46 gun down a road whilst an officer carrying field glasses signals to unseen soldiers behind the cameraman. This particular Russian weapon was based on the German 3.7cm Pak35/36, which weighed 510kg (1124Ibs) in action and fired a 1.43kg (3.15IB) shell that was capable of easily penetrating 38mm (1.50in) of armour at an angle of 30 degrees at a range of 1000m (1094yds).

Dressed in summer uniforms, including *pilotka* side caps, Soviet troops make slow progress in an advance against German troops on the Steppe. The soldiers on the left are hauling a Maxim 1919 machine gun toward the front lines.

Out on the Steppe Russian sappers were kept busy removing and collecting German anti-tank mines. The German laid thousands of mines along the Stalingrad Front that consequently posed a problem to the movement of the Soviet Army.

Two rare photographs showing an 8.8cm flak gun in action firing shells inside the city centre of Stalingrad. These German gunners belonging to the Luftwaffe's 9th Flak Division set up their deadly flak weapons in strategic areas of the city and pounded targets into rubble. In the second photo the dismounted limber can be seen next to the flak gun, just as a precautionary measure that the crew needed to hastily reposition the gun. Note the unhampered access to the ammunition

Out on the Steppe in a wheat field and German soldiers can be seen in what became commonly known as a machine gun nest. In the distance plumes of smoke rise into the air after two Russian T–34 tanks have been hit. Note the optical sight of the

During the battle of Stalingrad and indeed throughout the rest of the war the Red Army made full use of a variety of artillery ranging from mortars to howitzers, like this 76mm anti-tank gun.

In action is an 8.8cm Flak 36 which can be seen firing rounds into the northern outskirts of Stalingrad. Though the weapon was considered reasonably effective, actually moving the gun through the city was often awkward. However, where the terrain was frequently flat and open, like the Steppe, it allowed the long range performance of the gun to be decisive.

Soldiers take a much needed respite in a gully on the outskirts of Stalingrad. Note the 10.5cm leFH.18 light field howitzer being limbered next to a knocked out T–34 Russian tank. During October resistance by the Russian 62nd Army remained very strong and German forces reaching the Volga were becoming increasingly bogged down in merciless fighting.

An 8.8cm Flak 18 gun being prepared for action against targets around the grain silo factory in Stalingrad. This tall building which can be seen in the distance was one of the most heavily defended buildings in the city. In this huge grain elevator, south of the Tsaritsa Gorge, the fighting was unceasing. Note the sea of devastation around the building.

A photograph of a gutted building captured by the 389th Infantry Division at the end of October 1942. Though a number of areas in the centre of the city had been captured the Germans were now drawn into a heavy protracted battle of massive proportions. Soldiers would regularly spend whole days clearing a street, from one end to the other, to prepare for another battle the next day.

Three very interesting photographs showing German aerial reconnaissance pictures of fires raging following heavy Luftwaffe attacks on the city's oil storage yard on the Volga, north of the town centre. These photographs not only show the full extent of the fires but also the size of the city itself.

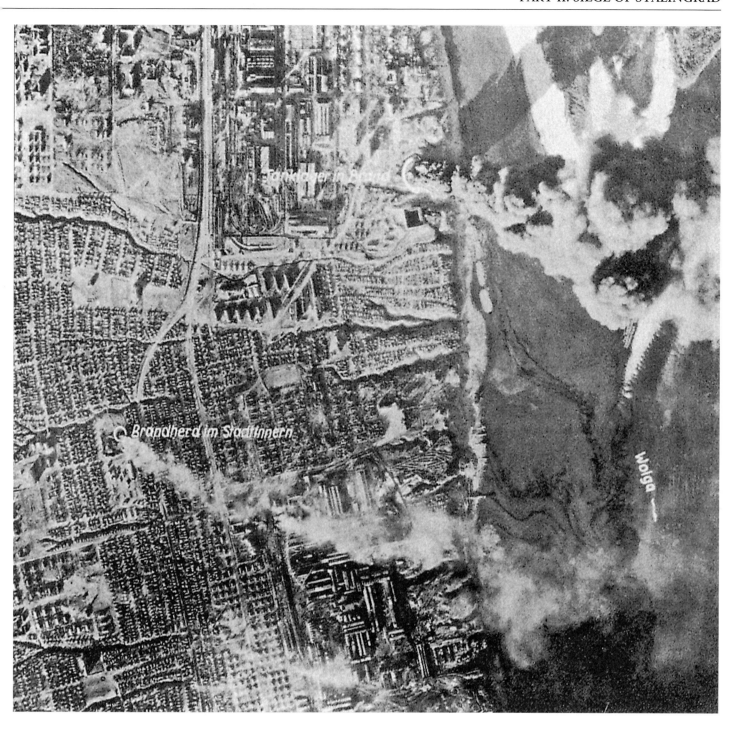

PART III

The Fall of Stalingrad

Desperation

On 11 December, the 6th Army war diary noted its first victims of death from malnutrition and exposure to sub-zero temperatures. Many now suffered from hepatitis and dysentery, and the first traces of blood were often a death sentence. Out of fear of frostbite most men wrapped themselves up with thick cloth, and never dared to wash or remove any of their clothing. One soldier wrote that 'there was no escape from this hell – save death itself.' In an attempt to compensate for the severe shortages of food a few tiny bits of horsemeat sometimes reached the troops. But not even these meagre amounts managed to compensate for their hunger. Instead, most fought on half starved in their miserable, cold and filthy trenches.

Whilst Paulus did what he could to try and alleviate the terrible conditions inside Stalingrad, news reached his command post that Manstein's relief attack had finally begun in earnest in the grey predawn light on 12 December. 'Operation Winter Storm' was spearheaded by General Kirchner's LVII *Panzer* Corps, consisting of the 6th *Panzer* Division, which was bolstered by some 160 tanks and 40 self-propelled guns, and the mauled 23rd *Panzer* Division. Protecting the *Panzer* corps flanks were Rumanian troops and two weak cavalry divisions.

During the first few uneasy days of the attack the panzers steadily rolled forward, making good progress over the light snow. But despite this auspicious beginning Manstein's forces were up against strong resilient opponents. On the second day of the operation the LVII *Panzer* Corps reached the Aksay River and captured the bridge at Zalivskiy. With heavy *Luftwaffe* support the advance moved progressively, but Manstein's forces still had another 45 miles to cover before it reached the pocket. On 17 December the LVII *Panzer* Corps increased to three divisions by the arrival of the 17th *Panzer* Division. With this added strength Kirchner pushed his forces hard across the snow, fighting bitterly as they advanced. Around the town of Kumsky, halfway between the Aksay and Mishkova Rivers, the corps became bogged down in a morass of heavy protracted fighting against two strong Russian mechanized corps and two tank brigades. It seemed that Manstein's fervent attempt to reach the *Kessel* and so relieve Paulus at Stalingrad was slowly slipping from his grasp. On 18 December with the cream of his armour burning and his troops fighting to break through what became known as the Aksay Line, the Field Marshal wearily sent a message to General Kurt Zeitzler of the Army High Command requesting him, 'to take immediate steps to initiate the breakout of the 6th Army towards the 4th *Panzer* Army'. The following day Manstein spoke to Hitler on the telephone pleading with him to rescind his order to stand fast, and allow the 6th Army to break out. But Manstein's efforts had been useless. Hitler, resolute as ever, refused his Field Marshal's pleas point blank. Putting down the receiver Manstein now knew that this mass of infantry of over a quarter of a million men would be totally annihilated if they were left there. On 21 December Manstein reported to Hitler that the 4th *Panzer* Army had advanced within 30 miles from Stalingrad, but the resistance from the enemy was so great that it could make no more progress. There was also no more fuel for the vehicles and without adequate supplies they were doomed to failure. Hitler had been initially encouraged by the success of the 4th *Panzer* and had ordered the *SS Panzergrenadier Division Wiking* to be transferred from Army Group A to support the Army's drive to Stalingrad, but it was already too late.

On Christmas Eve under merciless Russian attack the 4th *Panzer* Army was ordered to withdraw behind the Aksay River. As German units evacuated the area east of the river, more Russian reinforcements poured across the Volga armed with fresh infantry and new tanks, and replaced the exhausted units holding the foothills on the western banks. From their well fortified positions the Russians continued to use a variety of weaponry to hamper the survival of German soldiers trapped inside the pocket. Between 22 November and 23 December the 6th Army alone had lost some 28,000 men. The army reported just before Christmas that the remaining strength inside the pocket was 246,000, including 13,000 Rumanians, 19,300 Russian auxiliaries, and 6,000 wounded. Though the total strength appeared impressive, many of the soldiers were in poor shape and lacked sufficient weapons and ammunition. The combat effectiveness of the troops was further reduced by exhaustion and exposure, which according to a German pathologist that was flown in to the pocket to perform autopsies, found that shrinking of the heart and changes in the internal organs had resulted in many of the deaths. Visiting the troops the pathologist found that many of them were living in inadequate shelters and not properly clothed for the arctic conditions in which they had to endure. Their slender rations of bread, soup, and occasional horsemeat and the lack of medical supplies, were all progressively reducing the army's chance of survival. Those soldiers that were still fit enough to fight were often curtailed by bad weather. Between the Don and Volga rivers the weather varied considerably. Driving rain, thick snow, and fog perpetually delayed the conduct of operations.

All over the *Kessel* and inside Stalingrad itself the Russians continued to wage a relentless battle of attrition. At midnight on Christmas Eve the Red Army celebrated the holy season for several minutes with a massive artillery bombardment directed on every ensnared unit trapped inside the city. Under the constant hammer blows of artillery shells, soldiers sat huddled together shivering in their stinking dugouts, watching the snow rise and their comrades die. Many had little to do other than to think about the frostbite and watch the rats chewing on dead corpses in no man's land.

During the early hours of Christmas day, following a night of relative quiet, Stalingrad and the rest of the *Kessel* once more reverberated to the clatter of machine gun fire and the audible sounds of shells slamming onto pulverized German positions. As the frozen ground shook under the cannonade of thousands of *Katyusha* rockets, which screamed with all their fury, Red infantry loomed up in the smoke and attacked their enemy with fanatical violence. As quick as the attack began, it suddenly petered out. All that was heard among the soft sounds of the groaning wounded and the howling wind was a monotonous voice relayed over Russian loud speakers: "Every seven seconds a German soldier dies in Russia. Stalingrad – mass grave."

Christmas day for the soldiers in Stalingrad was sombre. Those strong enough to bring some kind of festive cheer in the trenches and bunkers sung their favourite carol, *Stille Nacht, heilige Nacht*. It was a very moving moment for many. In some areas where the lines were not under direct fire the men were able to pick from their shortwave radios the Christmas broadcast of *Grossdeutsche Rundfunk*, and huddle around to listen. To their amazement they heard a voice say, "This is Stalingrad from the Volga". Then a choir began singing, *Stille Nacht, heilige Nacht*. Whilst some troops accepted the deception in order to help raise morale, others however, felt enraged that their loved ones and the German people themselves had been purposely duped.

The scene along the Volga was far removed from anything associated with Christmas festivities. The temperature had fallen to minus 25 degrees. To keep up their spirits, some decorated their permanent positions in the frozen rubble with little Christmas trees. Huddled together with mud and filth around their ankles, they sat there listening to the endless wailing of the wounded and dying men, praying that the new year would bring them fresh hope and 'get them out of this hell.' But their Christmas wishes were never granted. Many of the troops had not eaten for forty-eight hours and the strength of the men was rapidly decreasing. The agony of actually starving to death was a constant preoccupation that every soldier thought about, and Christmas day only increased that awareness.

On 26 December food supplies had run so low that there was now only enough bread for two days. The ration of bread was then reduced to 120 grams and then halved. Each man would be supplied with soup but without fat or luncheon. Where food had completely run out in some areas of the front, there were stories of soldiers actually seen picking the oats out of their excrement, and in some circumstances, even eating the ripped warm flesh of their dead comrades before it froze. Many of the men were now too weak to dig for fresh emplacements. When they were forced under fire to leave their positions, they would simply huddle up behind heaped snow, numb with cold, waiting for the inevitability of being either frozen to death in the rubble, or killed by a sniper. When a soldier had been injured out in no man's land, stretcher bearers were often too weak to lift their dying comrade on to the stretcher to safety. Consequently, the stranded wounded were regularly left to die in the snow.

Paulus complained to Manstein that his army was 'on the brink of extinction.' Stalingrad, he said had become a graveyard. Hitler was warned about the appalling situation, but he believed that the 6th Army was safe inside its 'fortress', and could hold-out until the spring of 1943. He had ordered Goring to increase the air supply to at least 300-tons a day, and thought that this would be sufficient for the 6th Army to survive. But the situation was far worse than Hitler could ever have imagined. His 6th Army was slowly being starved to death. The *Kessel* had become littered with thousands of dead, and those still holding out were edging towards total obliteration.

Attacking the *Kessel*

By the end of 1942 the Russians had brilliantly executed their plans of sealing the fate of the 6th Army and breaking up Manstein's attempt to reach the trapped forces. The original success of the battle was mainly attributed to Soviet armour, and not the infantry. In many of the clashes with the Germans when odds were even, Russian troops showed itself to be distinctly inferior. In fact, although the 6th Army was now dying a lingering death from starvation and exhaustion its force still processed small advantages against their enemy. One of the main advantages was that in and around Stalingrad the *Kessel* was heavily built-up and troops had some shelter. This meant that survival was far greater than if it had to defend the flat and often treeless steppe between the Don and Volga Rivers. As a consequence the Soviets did not have the crushing effect that they initially expected, and quite regularly during the fighting inside the city they lost momentum. The results were often catastrophic, with many thousands of soldiers being killed or wounded. It seemed that the Russians too were paying a very high price in blood for Stalingrad.

For the first stage of the final attack the Red Army prepared to wipe out the Germans at Stalingrad. General Hoth's 4th *Panzer* Army did what it could by fighting a series of desperate battles against superior Russian forces to try and keep open a corridor through to Stalingrad. At its nearest point leading units were still only twenty miles from the 6th Army perimeter, but the Red Army had already driven the main force back some sixty miles below Kotelnikovo.

The first bitter days of 1943 opened up as had 1942 – with the German Army facing total catastrophe on the Eastern Front. In the south, where the Germans and allies had deployed the flower of their forces six months before, they were now weakening daily. The Germans exhausted by huge losses, saw a virtually intact Hungarian Army stretching along the Don as probably the only Axis partner capable now of holding the Russians in 'check'. Along a greatly extended defence line, the Germans supplied the Hungarians with as much equipment as could be mustered.

The Russians were fully aware that the Germans were still very powerful within the pocket, in spite of their weakened condition. The process of actually defeating them had been equally costly in terms of lives and material. By early January the weather, hunger, and fatigue had also taken a heavy toll on the Russians. General Rokossovsky commander of the Don Front wanted to avoid further bloodshed and called upon the Germans to surrender. On the morning of 8 January 1943, three Russian representatives carrying a white flag walked through the German lines and delivered the ultimatum to Paulus. The ultimatum stated that unless the Germans ceased hostilities and surrendered by ten o'clock on the morning of 9 January, "the Red Army and Air Force will be compelled to wipe out the surrounded German troops." Although Paulus was fully aware of the dire situation he did not want to surrender his army. He submitted the Russian ultimatum to Hitler, and again pleaded for freedom of action. The *Führer* refused once more and told Paulus that it was imperative that his army held out for as long as possible, as it was helping the entire front. Plans were still being drawn-up for a new relief expedition and three new panzer divisions were being moved from France, but they would not arrive until February. Paulus now knew that it would take a miracle to save the 6th Army from destruction.

Whilst *Führer* headquarters debated on the crises at Stalingrad and ways to relieve the 6th Army from its entombment, the Russians prepared to wipe out the pocket once and for all. All along the southern and western sides of the pocket the cold dawn of 10 January was suddenly broken by Russian gunnery officers giving the order for their men to begin a massive artillery barrage into the pocket. Hundreds of light, medium, and heavy guns, howitzers, and multiple-rockets launchers poured a hurricane of fire and destruction onto German positions. Shell after shell, rocket after rocket thundered into the pocket. Fearing complete annihilation of their positions some German troops frantically scrambled out of their burning trenches, but were immediately consumed by heavy shelling. The sky blackened from smoke and heat. The acrid gases from exploding shells blinded the eyes. The soldiers were deafened by the thunder of the guns. To the German soldier in this battle, it was unlike any other engagement they had previously encountered. As German units tried to hold their disintegrating lines Russian infantry moved forward into action supported by hundreds of T–34 tanks that burst through the perimeter in the middle of the front. The attack was so fierce that the German 376th and 384th divisions were engulfed by the Red Army and totally annihilated.

In the southwest the German 29th Motorized and 3rd Motorized division tried to hold, but were mercilessly battered by strong Russian infantry supported by masses of armour. The 3rd Motorized Division was forced to withdraw across the Rossoshka River with serious losses. The 29th Motorized Division after fighting off heavy attacks retreated across the steppe littered with burning vehicles and dead corpses towards Stalingrad.

Both the Germans and the remnants of their allies suffered enormous casualties. The Hungarian 7th Division endured a hideous battle which resulted in their total destruction. The Red Army continued mounting further

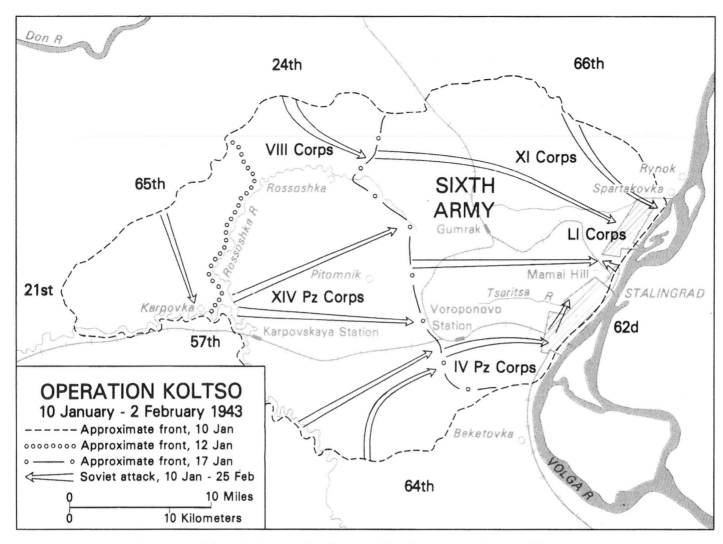

Operation Koltso, 10 January-2 February 1943, the Soviet reduction of Stalingrad
(map appears courtesy of the Center of Military History United States Army, and originally appeared on page 498 of
Moscow to Stalingrad: Decision in the East by Earl F. Ziemke & Magna E. Bauer, 1987)

attacks on other Hungarian and German divisions. Once again, bewildered soldiers were thrown into the front lines only to be confronted with a wall of fire. Soon whole groups of them were either blasted into oblivion or forced to retreat. Often in the confusion many men ran the wrong way, straight into the enemy, only to be mown down or captured and tortured to death. Within a week, the Hungarians had lost more than 96,000 killed, missing or wounded. The German 76th Division had now been reduced from 10,000 men to only 600. The Red Army had demolished the western side of the *Kessel* to about 250 square miles and had been pushed to within five miles of Paulus's headquarters, Gumark, and Stalingrad was no more than ten miles away. To defend these western approaches and form a defensive line north to south in front of Stalingrad, the 113th and 297th divisions, 14th *Panzer* and 9th Flak divisions, along with exhausted remnants of six divisions were thrown into the twenty mile defence line. For five long days the troops shivered and died of exposure on the steepe, too weak to dig a fox hole or a dugout. Most of them just sat around huddling together waiting for yet another merciless artillery bombardment from the Russians. From the west the Russians continued to fight bitterly. Thousands of Red Army troops and tanks spewed forth heralding the final onslaught against the pocket's western front. Defending these positions were starving men, sometimes too cold to even hold or fire their weapons. But despite the terrible situation and dwindling resources the German batteries and battalions fought on to the bitter death. Frantically those that were able to retreat, struggled eastwards in desperate flight towards Stalingrad. As the Russians remorselessly pushed on, Paulus and his staff evacuated their headquarters and retreated into Stalingrad to set up a new command post.

Destruction of the 6th Army

The Red Army now pushed ever closer to Stalingrad from the west and bit by bit they captured and destroyed hundreds of pillboxes and other German strong points. By 17 January the Russians reported that they had destroyed some 1,260 pillboxes and fortified dugouts, including 75 heavily defended observation posts and 317 gun emplacements. They had also captured or destroyed 400 aircraft, more than 600 tanks, and around 16,000 trucks. Twenty-five thousands German had been killed and several thousand prisoners taken, many of which were Rumanians. The Red Army was unstoppable and it seemed only a matter of time before the 6th Army was completely destroyed.

On 22 January Gumrak, the last airfield, fell as the Russians tore a three mile gap in the southwestern sector. With no fuel and a serious lack of guns and ammunition to repel the Soviets the 6th Army was unable to close the gap. The following day the Red Army broke through the western perimeter and leading units penetrated German positions all the way to the tractor works. The Russian drive into Stalingrad was so swift that it actually cut the pocket in two and isolated the XI Corps to the north. A weary and exhausted Paulus reported that there were more than 12,000 unattended wounded, many of whom were just lying in the streets or inside ruined buildings. Hitler ordered Paulus not to surrender under any cost and instructed him that only those capable of fighting would now be fed. Fighting was hopeless and despite stiff resistance in some areas nothing could be done to avert the inevitable destruction of the 6th Army. The chief of operations of the 6th Army sent a message to Manstein to explain the dire situation.

> Attacks in undiminished strength are continually being made against the entire western front which has been fighting its way back eastward to the Gorodische area since the morning of the 24th in order to form a hedgehog in the tractor works. In the southern part of Stalingrad the western front along the city outskirts held on to the western and southern edges of Minima until 4 P.M. Local penetrations were made in this area. The Volga and northeastern fronts are unchanged. The conditions inside the city are terrible, where twenty-thousand unattended wounded need sheltering in the ruins. Among the wounded are many starving and frostbitten men and stragglers, with many without weapons, which they lost during the battle. Heavy artillery is destroying the city. Along the outskirts of the city in the southern part of Stalingrad a last ditch resistance is being offered on 25 January under the courageous leadership of our Generals and gallant officers. It may be possible that the tractor works will hold out a little longer.

For those soldiers fighting inside Stalingrad, a mood of despair and dread gripped them as never before. Much of the 6th Army was starving. Paulus's army was now broken up into two pockets and conditions were appalling. The soldiers that no longer had the energy and willpower to fight sought shelter in the dark and dank cellars and basements of the ruined buildings. Here in unimaginable horror and torment the sick, frostbitten, wounded and dying soldiers lay packed together. All of them had either, dysentery, tetanus, spotted fever, typhus, pneumonia or gangrene. Up above, across the fire-raked devastation, the rest of the 6th Army was slowly being incinerated in the inferno. Paulus himself was now a General riddled with dysentery, and close to reaching a nervous breakdown. His headquarters was now situated in the ruins of a large department store in Red Square, defended by what was left of General Hartmann's 71st Infantry Division. Laying on his camp bed beneath his gutted command post, his thoughts went out to the brave men that had fought with undiminished courage against overwhelming superior forces.

Whilst the last remaining pockets of the 6th Army were being blown to pieces by point blank Russian artillery, Hitler showered promotions on the 6th Army's senior officers. Paulus was given supreme honour and promoted to Field Marshal, knowing very well that no German soldier of that rank had ever surrendered. Unaware of his *Führer's* ulterior motive of wanting him to either die fighting or commit suicide than surrender to the Russians, the newly decorated Field Marshal sent a dignified response of his burning allegiance to Hitler:

> On the anniversary of your accession to power, the 6th Army sends greetings to its Führer. The swastika flag still flutters over Stalingrad. Should our struggle be an example to present and future generations never to surrender, even when all hope is gone, then Germany will be victorious. *Heil, Mein Führer!"*

During that day heavy fighting intensified as Red Army forces began overwhelming the last German defensive positions. The 76th Infantry Division was surrounded and forced to surrender. Near the railway station number 1, the headquarters of the XIV *Panzer* Corps was also compelled to capitulate. In the northern pocket Russian T–34's had smashed their way through and decimated hundreds of German troops. Within a matter of hours the command bunkers of the VIII and LI corps were captured. Generals Sydlitz, Heitz, and five other Generals reluctantly surrendered. The Russians then attacked the 71st Infantry and during the vicious street fighting General Hartmann was killed. Soviet troops were also closing in on Paulus's command post.

On the morning of 31 January at 6.15, the radio operator in Paulus's headquarters sent a frantic message: "The Russian are at the door. We are preparing to destroy the radio equipment." The radio then went dead. Minutes later a German officer climbed out of the command post and waved a white flag to approaching Russian soldiers. Paulus had finally surrendered.

Two days later at 8.40 in the morning of 2 February the last German pocket in Stalingrad finally surrendered. General Strecker's XI Corps had fought courageously for days but was unable to avert the situation decisively. As Strecker's exhausted and starved men shuffled pitifully through the snow into captivity, the Russians rejoiced. The battle of Stalingrad, the most protracted and bloodiest battle of the war, had finally come to an abrupt end.

A German soldier is using a trench periscope. The periscope was an optical device for conducting observations from a concealed protected position. The device was very effective especially during the battle of Stalingrad where soldiers often had to endure many hours or even days in the same trench or fortified position.

An infantryman exits one of many destroyed buildings in the city. Movement on foot across the city, especially on exposed ground could be lethal during combat. As a result sewers were used, or trenches were dug, to enable infantry to safely move from one building to another.

Here a group of German soldiers rest during a lull in the fighting. On 9 October German troops began digging in and awaiting reinforcements. The 6th Army communiqué stated that day that there was no heavy fighting to report in the city.

During a pause in the fighting the crew of a 5cm Pak 38 anti-tank gun move their weapon into main street to ward off any Red Army counterattacks. The Pak 38 was well liked among the crews that had the chance to use it in battle. Not only was the weapon effective in combat, but also easy to conceal.

On the outskirts of Stalingrad near the workers housing area a soldier fires a MG–34 machine gun. In his possession the soldier is also armed with a Mauser Kar.98k carbine and a captured Russian PPSh–41 submachine gun. This captured submachine gun, nicknamed by the Russians as the 'Finka', was widely used by the German Army in Stalingrad. It was rugged, reliable, and had a large magazine capacity.

A machine gun troop has halted in a main street in the heart of Stalingrad. One of the soldiers can clearly be seen holding a captured map probably of the city. Although this area of Stalingrad had been captured, moving through it was still perilous. A great many of the approaches into the city were still heavily mined and sappers would often lay in wait.

A 5cm Pak 38 anti-tank gun crew pause during intensive street fighting inside the city. The crew has interestingly tried to disguise the gun by adding camouflaging to it with pieces of wreckage found in the street. Camouflage netting too has been wrapped around the 5cm gun barrel as well. The Pak 38 was used extensively during the battle of Stalingrad and became a very

A Russian T–34 tank has been knocked out of action and lies on its side along the banks of the Volga. The T–34 tank was built in vast quantities and was used widely against German forces around Stalingrad with devastating effect.

On the outskirts of the city a Red Army gun crew prepares to fire yet another salvo from their 122mm M1939 howitzer deep into German positions. Although this howitzer was not very effective in urbanized combat its crews were able to pulverize enemy targets from the edge of the city with devastating effects.

A German soldier tucking into rations whilst inside a shelter on the Volga. By the end of October the 6th Army were beginning to show signs of frustration and fatigue. Food supplies too were also dwindling at an alarming rate.

Two photographs showing Russian troops surrendering to German troops. By the end of October Red Army positions had been pulverized into a few remaining pockets of resistance. Though General Paulus expressed confidence in winning the battle of Stalingrad, winter was fast approaching, giving a new dimension to the horrific conditions that the soldiers had to endure. German difficulties soon multiplied as news reached the 6th Army that large Russian formations were bearing down on

Outside Stalingrad two soldiers can be seen with a medical box. These men are more than likely attached to a medical corps, and behind them their Sd.Kfz.251 halftrack displays the Red Cross on the side of the vehicle's armour.

Here a medic gives a soldier first aid treatment and after bandaging his upper left arm he assists by carefully helping with his tunic. By early November casualty rates in and around Stalingrad had risen dramatically. It had been estimated that more than 50,000 German soldiers had been injured in action and only a limited amount were fit enough to return for front line

In the suburbs of Stalingrad and German troops examine a captured *Katyusha* multiple rocket launcher platform. The Katyusha was designed to fire 42.5kg (93.6Ib) rockets into German-held positions. It was not a precision weapon, but precision was not really necessary when a battery of rocket launchers were able to drop more than 2,400kg (5,280Ib) of explosive onto the target.

German commanders stand next to a Ju–52 transport aircraft before it resumes its mission supplying the beleaguered 6th Army. Three of the men can be seen wearing fur caps. These items of headgear were not official issue but the German Army wore them during the second winter on the Eastern Front. The men are wearing the cap with side flap down, in order to keep the wearer's ears warm in the cold.

A Romanian soldier has been killed during heavy fighting on the steppe. For the Romanians fighting south of Stalingrad, the battlefield resembled conditions like those fought in the First World War. Though they attempted in a number of areas to hold the front they were manifestly incapable of serious resistance as the Red Army was far superior in strength. Consequently, a mood of fear and despair gripped them as whole units were either blasted into oblivion or forced to retreat

Two soldiers move along a dirt road on the outskirts of the city. Both men are wearing the greatcoat, which was the most common winter garment issued during the first winter period of the war in Russia. Under the greatcoat they are more than likely wearing the standard field service uniform tucked into the traditional long shaft leather marching boots. Their winter clothing consists of woolen toques under the field cap and thick woolen gloves. Worn over the greatcoat is the usual rifleman's equipment and weapons including the leather belt and ammunition pouches.

An infantry gun crew with their 7.5cm le.IG 18 out on the steppe in early November 1942. These small light highly mobile infantry guns were more than capable of providing German troops with vital offensive and defensive fire support, particularly when heavier artillery was unavailable.

German troops south of Stalingrad during a lull in the fighting. A whitewashed 7.5cm le.IG gun can be seen being towed by animal draught. The gun was widely used on the Eastern Front and remained the standard light infantry gun throughout the war. The Germans generally assigned light field guns or pack howitzers to dedicated infantry fire support, though still remaining under artillery control.

A soldier on the shores of the Volga next to a captured Russian trench. Many of these captured trenches were used by the Germans, which remained their homes until the final days of the battle of Stalingrad.

Defending their positions inside a bomb crater troops are heavily embroiled in fighting. By mid-November the cold was so bad that weapon actions frequently froze. To make matters worse insufficient supplies were reaching the men inside the doomed city. Consequently, many soldiers were without adequate winter clothing which exposed thousands of men to the dangers of frostbite and freezing to death.

Outside the city troops use straw in a vain attempt not only to camouflage their vehicle from aerial observation, but to protect it from the freezing night time temperatures. The arctic weather caused constant problems for the Germans. Vehicles would not start for the battery plates were warped, cylinder blocks cracked, or crankshafts and axles refused to turn. Precious fuel too would regularly have to be burned beneath the engines in a desperate attempt to thaw out engines.

A machine gun crew tuck into their rations during a pause in the fighting on the steppe. The soldiers are wearing the snow overall. This white garment was an early piece of snow clothing. It was long, which covered the entire service uniform. It was shapeless and had buttons right down the front and had a deep collar, an attached hood and long sleeves. The infantryman's leather belt and personal equipment was worn attached around the outside of the garment in order to allow better access.

German troops move along a road with supplies bound for the Volga on 11 November 1942. It was on this day in freezing temperatures that the 6th Army launched its final attack in Stalingrad, code-named 'Hubertus'. Many of the troops however were hungry, exhausted, lice ridden and suffering from dysentery. Conditions were appalling, but the Germans still attacked, inflicting a great many casualties on the Red Army.

A soldier inside Stalingrad armed with an MP–40 submachine gun. By the end of November the 6th Army was completely encircled. Hitler had issued orders that Paulus's force should make no attempt to break out from Stalingrad, assuring the General that the *Luftwaffe* would supply his trapped army from the air.

A machine gun troop have halted on a road near Stalingrad. None of the soldiers have received winter camouflage smocks making them easy targets against enemy snipers and machine gun posts. Furthermore, Russian aircraft too could easily identify German soldiers dressed in regular uniforms and advancing across the snow.

A whitewashed Ju–52 transport plane has landed at a snow covered airstrip bringing supplies to the 6th Army. Despite desperate measures to supply the 6th Army the *Luftwaffe* not only have insufficient aircraft to undertake such an immense operation, but only six of the airstrips around Stalingrad could be operated by day. The only airfield inside the Stalingrad pocket able to cope with the large scale operations was Pitomnik.

Inside the Stalingrad *Kessel* at Pitomnik soldiers have loaded fuel drums onboard a truck. For weeks the 6th Army had suffered critical shortages of fuel and as a result many vehicles simply broke down and were abandoned. Paulus required a staggering 250,000 gallons of fuel, almost 10 times the quantity that had been already delivered by air.

A photograph has captured the moment a sIG.33 artillery gun is fired during operation 'Winter Storm'. The operation was unleashed on 12 December 1942 by troops of Group Hoth, including elite units of the *Waffen SS*. At first the attack went well, but within a matter of a couple of days the Germans encountered fierce resistance from the Soviet 5th Shock Army.

Manstein's relief operation and *Panzergrenadiers* hitch a lift on board a whitewashed Pz.Kpfw.III bound for the Stalingrad pocket. The Germans had a sixty-mile march to the southern edge of the pocket. Although the drive went well initially bad weather coupled with low visibility grounded vital Luftwaffe support. When the column reached the Aksai River, Panzer crews found that the river was only solid enough to carry foot soldiers, not tanks.

A 15cm howitzer crew from Group Hoth deploys their gun against Russian forces blocking their path towards the Stalingrad pocket. By 21 December advanced German units had managed to push within 30 miles of the Stalingrad pocket and reported that they could see smoke and explosions coming from the pocket.

An artillery crew pose for the camera during a lull in the fighting outside the Stalingrad pocket in December 1942. Despite desperate attempts by the 4th *Panzer* Army to reach the pocket it was unable to make any more progress due to being constantly heavily engaged by Russian tanks and infantry.

Support vehicles belonging to the 4th *Panzer* Army have halted in the snow after the leading column has come under heavy attack. The 4th *Panzer* Army not only had to deal with heavy enemy resistance but the extreme arctic temperatures and deep snow caused unprecedented problems, especially for non-tracked vehicles.

At one of the dressing stations on the Volga and a German officer poses for the camera with his right hand heavily bandaged. Inside the city itself the wounded were left untreated in cellars and destroyed buildings. Those that could not be stretchered to relative safety were often left stranded in the snow to die.

During Manstein's relief operation and a halftrack has developed a mechanical problem. One of the crew members can be seen with the engine cover open. Note the foul weather cover over the crew compartment.

Infantrymen trudge through the snow north of Aksai. Despite frantic attempts to relieve the 6th Army Manstein's force was halted by well prepared enemy positions that made it almost impossible for infantry and tanks to advance. On 18 December, with most of Manstein's armour burning and his troops fighting to break through the Askai Line, von Manstein wearily sent a message to the Army High Command requesting that the 6th Army make immediate steps to initiate a breakout of

Soldiers prepare to move to another position within the city. By December one of the main weaknesses of the German soldier at Stalingrad was his tendency to avoid close combat, and a belief that the tanks must advance before infantry would move.

During heavy fighting inside the city a MG–34 machine gun can be seen mounted on a Dreifuss anti-aircraft tripod mounting. The soldier appears to be wearing a sheepskin coat and a captured Russian shapka-ushanka cap.

During fighting on the steppe near the Don River a MG–34 machine gunner positions his weapon on a bipod inside a bomb crater. During January 1943 Red Army troops were pressing against the thinning German front lines circling the city. German troops and their allies left on the steppe were trying frantically to prevent the enemy from crushing their forces and destroying the 6th Army trapped inside the city.

A rare chance to see Cossacks advancing on Stalingrad in January 1943. Although the Cossacks were vulnerable to modern automatic weapons, they were self-reliant and very effective on the battlefield, especially against ill-equipped enemy units. The Cossacks were also successfully utilized for anti-partisan activity in the German Army rear areas.

A photograph taken during the last weeks of the battle of Stalingrad showing German officers posing in front of their command post, which was set up in a tunnel overlooking the banks of the frozen Volga.

Epilogue

When the last of Field-Marshal Paulus's troops finally surrendered on 2 February 1943 the Red Army found it hard to believe that the battle of Stalingrad had come to an end and that they were victorious. As the gaunt prisoners emerged crawling from the cellars, dugouts, and bunkers, with their hands held high in surrender, the Russians noticed that many of the men had suffered frostbite and could hardly walk. They also observed that the Rumanian soldiers were in a worse shape than their German allies. According to the Rumanians, their meagre rations had been stopped in an attempt to maintain German strength. As a consequence the loss of life was huge. The Rumanians had lost 173,000 killed, wounded, and missing, of which a quarter had perished through malnutrition and the arctic temperatures. The Croatian expeditionary force had been totally destroyed, including the 369th Regiment which had been wiped out by Russian troops at Stalingrad. The Italians had lost 115,000 dead and wounded, with 66,000 missing, of which a high number probably drowned in the semi-frozen rivers that had cracked open when hundreds retreated across them.

As for the Germans their losses were equally immense. Some 150,000 Germans were killed, with 91,000 being taken into captivity, many of which were never to see their homeland again. During the fighting some 30,000 wounded were flown out of the ravaged city.

Russian losses were much higher than that of both the Germans and their allies. Although figures vary, more than 750,000 Red Army troops were killed and wounded. In five months of bitter and bloody fighting 99 percent of Stalingrad was destroyed and of the 500,000 inhabitants of the city, only 1,500 remained to endure the horror with many being caught up and killed in the battle.

Although the Russians paid a high price for their hard fought victory, the Germans had lost both an army and a very important campaign. Both the banks of the Don and the Volga were now littered with the dead and the ambitions of the once vaunted 6th Army had been destroyed. Although Hitler said that the 6th Army had provided a valuable service by tying down almost three quarters of a million enemy troops the loss of the campaign was so immense that it marked the turning point of the war in Russia. Never again was Hitler to launch a major offensive in Russia. His army was now faced with a relentlessly growing and improving Red Army.

APPENDIX I

German Personal Equipment and Weapons

The German soldier was very well equipped and in 1939, when the German war was unleashed against Europe, he was perhaps the best in the world. The rifleman or *Schütze* wore the trademark model 1935 steel helmet, which provided ample protection whilst marching to the battlefront and during combat. His leather belt with support straps carried two sets of three ammunition pouches for a total of 60 rounds for his rifle. The soldier also wore his combat harness for his mess kit and special camouflage rain cape or *Zeltbahn*. He also wore an entrenching tool, and attached to the entrenching tool carrier was the bayonet, a bread bag for rations, gas mask canister, which was invariably slung over the wearer's shoulder and an anti-gas cape in its pouch, attached to the shoulder strap. The infantryman's flashlight was normally attached to the tunic and inside the tunic pocket he carried wound dressings. A small backpack was issued to the soldiers, though some did not wear it. The backpack was intended for spare clothing, personal items, and additional rations along with a spare clothing satchel.

The weapons used by the German soldier varied, but the standard issue piece of equipment was the 7.92mm Kar98k carbine. This excellent modern and effective bolt-action rifle was of Mauser design. This rifle remained the most popular weapon used by the German Army throughout the war. Another weapon used by the German Army, but not to the same extent as the Kar98k, was the 9mm MP38 or MP40 machine pistol. This submachine gun was undoubtedly one of the most effective weapons ever produced for the German war machine. The 7.92mm MG34 light machine gun was yet another weapon that featured heavily within the ranks of the German Army. The effectiveness of the weapon made it the most superior machine gun ever produced at that time. The MG34 and later the MG42 possessed a very impressive fire rate and could dominate the battlefield both in defensive and offensive roles. The German Army possessed the MG34 in every rifle group, and machine gun crews were able to transport this relatively light weapon easily onto the battlefield by resting it over the shoulder. Yet another weapon, which was seen at both company and battalion level on the battlefield, was the 5cm 1.GrW36 light mortar and 8cm s. GrW34 heavy mortar. Although they could both be an effective weapon when fired accurately the light and heavy mortar were far too heavy and too expensive to produce on a very large scale.

At regimental and divisional level the German Army possessed its own artillery in the form of 7.5cm lIG18, 10.5cm lFH18, 15cm sFH18, and 15cm sIG33 infantry guns. Specially trained artillery crews used these guns and they were seen extensively in Poland, Western Front, Balkans, and the first two years of war in Russia. The 3.7cm Pak35/36 was another weapon that was very popular, especially during the early years of the war. However, by the time the German invasion of Russia was unleashed *Panzerjäger* crews were starting to become aware of the tactical limitations of the weapon.

APPENDIX II

Typical German Infantry Battalion, 1941 to 1942

Battalion Headquarters (5 officers, 27 men)

Communications Platoon (22 men)

Battalion Supply Train (32 men)

Machine Gun Company (5 officers, 197 men)

Company HQ (1 officer, 14 men)

Company Train (17 men)

Mortar Platoon (1 officer, 61 men)

3 Machine Gun Platoons, *each* (1 officer, 35 men)

3 Rifle Companies (4 officers, 187 men)

Company HQ (1 officer, 12 men)

Company Supply Train (24 men)

Anti-tank Rifle Section (7 men)

3 Rifle Platoons, each comprised of:

Platoon HQ (1 officer, 5 men)

Light Mortar Section (3 men)

Four Rifle Squads, each comprised of 10 men

Total Strength of 861 all ranks (22 officers and 839 men)

Combat Chronology of German 6th Army Eastern Front Campaign 1941–42

22 June–12 July 1941

Battles in Galicia and Volhynien

Battles between the Bug and the Styr river, and the Stalin Line

2 July 1941–25 July 1941

Drive to Kiev and to the Djniepr river

Breakthrough the Stalin Line

Battle near Cudnov – Berdischev and defensive battles near Zviahel and Sokolov.

14 July–21 August 1941

Battle north of Zhitomir

25 July–5 October 1941

Battles near the Djniepr and crossing the river

Driving the Red Army over the Djniepr river

Battle near Boguslav – Tscherkassy

Battle of Kiev

Battle for the bridgehead Gornostaipol – Ostjer

Encircling battle eastwards of the Dnjiepr

Battle east of Kiev

1 October–26 October 1941

Advance to the Donets River

Battle at Psiol and the Worskla river

Battle near Karkhov and Begorod

26 October 1941–29 June 1942

Battle at the higher Donets river and at Ssemina

Battle near Obojan and Rshawa

Defensive battle north of Karkhov

Battle at Karkhov [Operation Frediricus]

Defensive battle near Karkhov

Encircling battle southwest of Karkhov

Battle of Voltschansk

Battle of Isjum – Kupjansk

28 June–22 August 1942 (Summer Campaign Operation Blau)

Breakthrough and advance to the middle of the Don River

Battle at Kalatsji – Ostrovsky – Kletskaja

Reach the Volga River and the battle of Stalingrad commences

German 6th Army Order of Battle 1942

8 June 1942

XVII Corps
294 Infantry Division

XXIX Corps
75 Infantry Division
168 Infantry Division
57 Infantry Division

LI Corps
44 Infantry Division
297 Infantry Division
71 Infantry Division
62 Infantry Division

VIII Corps
336 Infantry Division
113 Infantry Division
305 Infantry Division
79 Infantry Division

XL (mot) Corps
23 Panzer Division
3 Panzer Division

III (mot) Corps
60 Infantry Division (mot)
22 Panzer Division
16 Panzer Division
14 Panzer Division
376 Infantry Division
108 Infantry Division
389 Infantry Division

24 June 1942

XVII Corps
294 Infantry Division
79 Infantry Division
113 Infantry Division

XXIX Corps
75 Infantry Division
168 Infantry Division
57 Infantry Division

VIII Corps
376 Infantry Division
389 Infantry Division
305 Infantry Division

XXXX (mot) Corps
23 Panzer Division
3 Panzer Division
29 Infantry Division (mot)
336 Infantry Division
100 (leichte) Infantry Division
Infantry Regiment 369 (Croatian)

4 July 1942

XVII Corps
294 Infantry Division
79 Infantry Division
113 Infantry Division

XXIX Corps
75 Infantry Division
168 Infantry Division
57 Infantry Division

LI Corps
44 Infantry Division
297 Infantry Division
71 Infantry Division
62 Infantry Division

VIII Corps
389 Infantry Division
376 Infantry Division
305 Infantry Division

XXXX (mot) Corps

23 Panzer Division
3 Panzer Division
100 (leichte) Infantry Division
336 Infantry Division
29 Infantry Division (mot)
376 Infantry Division
108 Infantry Division
389 Infantry Division

5 August 1942

XVII Corps

79 Infantry Division
3 Infantry Division 'Celere' (Italian)

XIV (mot) Corps

60 Infantry Division (mot)
16 Panzer Division
3 Infantry Division (mot)

LI Corps

44 Infantry Division
295 Infantry Division

VIII Corps

384 Infantry Division
376 Infantry Division
305 Infantry Division
113 Infantry Division

XXIV Corps

24 Panzer Division
297 Infantry Division
71 Infantry Division
76 Infantry Division

12 August 1942

XVII Corps

79 Infantry Division
3 Infantry Division 'Celere' (Italian)
22 Panzer Division
113 Infantry Division
6th Bersaglieri Regiment (Italian)

XIV Panzer-Korps

60 Infantry Division (mot)
16 Panzer Division
3 Infantry Division (mot)

LI Corps

44 Infantry Division
71 Infantry Division

XI Corps

100 Jager-Division
Infantry Regiment 369 (Croatian)

VIII Corps

384 Infantry Division
376 Infantry Division
305 Infantry Division
389 Infantry Division

XXIV Panzer-Korps

16 Infantry Division (mot)
295 Infantry Division

2 September 1942

XVII Corps

79 Infantry Division
113 Infantry Division
22 Panzer Division

XIV Panzer-Korps

60 Infantry Division (mot)
16 Panzer Division
3 Infantry Division (mot)
295 Infantry Division

LI Corps

71 Infantry Division
76 Infantry Division

VIII Corps

384 Infantry Division
389 Infantry Division
305 Infantry Division

XI Corps

44 Infantry Division
100 Jager-Division
376 Infantry Division

8 October 1942

VIII Romanian Corps

14th Infantry Division
5th Infantry Division
1st Armoured Division
6th Infantry Division
13th Infantry Division
1st Cavalry Division

XIV Panzer-Korps

60 Infantry Division (mot)
16 Panzer Division

3 Infantry Division (mot)
94 Infantry Division

LI Corps

389 Infantry Division
100 Jager-Division
24 Panzer Division
295 Infantry Division

VIII Corps

113 Infantry Division
305 Infantry Division

XI Corps

44 Infantry Division
384 Infantry Division
376 Infantry Division
71 Infantry Division
76 Infantry Division

19 November 1942

IV Corps

29 (mot) Infantry Division
297 Infantry Division
371 Infantry Division

VII Corps

76 Infantry Division
113 Infantry Division

XI Corps

44 Infantry Division
376 Infantry Division
384 Infantry Division

XIV Panzer-Korps

3 (mot) Infantry Division
60 (mot) Infantry Division
16 Panzer Division

LI Corps

71 Infantry Division
79 Infantry Division
94 Infantry Division
100 Jäger-Division
295 Infantry Division
305 Infantry Division
389 Infantry Division
14 Panzer Division
24 Panzer Division
9 Flak-Division

51 Mortar Regiment
53 Mortar Regiment
2 Nebelwerfer Regiment
30 Nebelwerfer Regiment
4 Artillery Regiment
46 Artillery Regiment
64 Artillery Regiment
70 Artillery Regiment
54 Artillery Battalion
616 Artillery Battalion
627 Artillery Battalion
849 Artillery Battalion
49 Heavy Artillery Battalion
101 Heavy Artillery Battalion
733 Heavy Artillery Battalion
6 Pioneer Battalion
41 Pioneer Battalion

APPENDIX V

Soviet Orders of Battle

17 July 1942

64th Army
29th Infantry Division
112th Infantry Division
214th Infantry Division
229th Infantry Division
783rd Infantry Regiment
804th Infantry Regiment
66th (Motorised) Naval Infantry Brigade
154th (Motorised) Naval Infantry Brigade
40th Armoured Brigade
137th Armoured Brigade
5 heavy tanks

October 1942

62nd Army
10th NKVD Rifle Division
2 x Independent Infantry Brigades
13th Guards Rifle Division
35th Guards Rifle Division
37th Guards Rifle Division (initially without anti-tank guns)
39th Guards Rifle Division
45th Rifle Division
95th Rifle Division
112th Rifle Division
138th Rifle Division
193rd Rifle Division
196th Rifle Division
244th Rifle Division
284th (Siberian) Rifle Division
308th (Siberian) Rifle Division
84th Tank Brigade
137th Tank Brigade
189th Tank Brigade
92nd Naval Infantry Brigade
42nd Special Brigade
115th Special Brigade
124th Special Brigade
140th Special Brigade
160th Special Brigade
8th Air Army

Bibliography

Beevor, A. *Stalingrad* (London: Viking, 1998)

Carell, P. *Stalingrad: the Defeat of the German 6th Army* (Atglen PA: Schiffer, 2004)

Einsiedel, H. Graf von et al *Stalingrad: Memories and Reassessments* (London: Cassell, 2002)

Erickson, J. *The Road to Stalingrad* (London: Phoenix, 2003)

Haupt, W. *Die deutschen Infanterie-Divisonen* (Eggolsheim: Nebel, 2000)

Kannapin, N. *Die deutsche Feldpostübersicht 1939–1945* (Osnabrück: Biblio, 1980–82, 3 Bde)

Schmitz, P. & K.-J. Thies *Die Truppenkennzeichen der Verbände und Einheiten der deutchen Wehrmacht und Waffen-SS* (Osnabrück: Biblio, 1987–2000, 4 Bde)

Ziemke, E.F. *Moscow to Stalingrad: Decision in the East* (New York: Hippocrene, 1989)

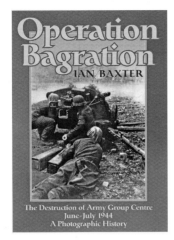